Are You Ready For Business?

Dave Shannon

THIS BOOK IS DEDICATED TO MY
AMAZING WIFE BECKY, MY WONDERFUL
KIDS, MEGAN AND OSCAR, AND TO MY
ALWAYS SUPPORTIVE PARENTS.

CONTENTS

ACKNOWLEDGMENTS

This book started as a lockdown project during the coronavirus pandemic. My wife continued to work in school whilst I worked from home and home schooled the kids. When I first had the idea of the book, I didn't know whether there was demand for such a book, but I went through the writing process anyway, and as more and more people read the book, the more I realised there was a need for it.

I'd like to thank Sarah Alcock, Chris Bensted, Lou Walsh, Gary Thompson, Daniel Hill, my parents and my wife for taking the time to read through the early versions of this book and who gave their feedback to help me make the final edit. As people who work in business, most of which are in the driving instructor industry, their thoughts and comments were very much appreciated and taken on board to create what you're holding in your hands today.

A big thank you must go out to my wife Becky who has always given her backing to everything I've wanted to do in business. She truly is my best friend and keeps me going when things get tough. She is also the creator of the name of my business and she will never let me forget that!

Thank you to my parents for always being there for me and my family. Your enthusiasm for everything I do is greatly appreciated.

I also need to thank my wonderful children, Megan and Oscar, who are always very patient with me when I'm trying to get things done. They're great kids and everything I do is to try and provide the best future for them (even if I can be a bit grumpy when I'm trying to get things done)!

Last but certainly not least, thank you to my nephew Joel who created the front cover for this book. He's still in high school at the moment but is already an excellent artist. Check out his Facebook page Joel Walley Art to see his amazing creations!

INTRODUCTION

If you're reading this, then I assume you fall into one of these 3 categories:

- an Approved Driving Instructor (ADI)
- a Potential Driving Instructor (PDI)
- someone who's thinking of becoming a driving instructor

Whichever of these categories you fall into then this book is for you. When you train to become a driving instructor, you'll spend hour upon hour honing your skills to become proficient in delivering driving lessons.

You learn how to become a driving instructor –

however, did anyone teach you how to be a business owner?

I'll be clear from the start; this book gives no advice

or training relating to driving instruction. This book will help you to be better at business. Whether you choose to work on your own or with another driving school on a franchise basis, you will be running your own business. Personally, I've experienced it from every angle. I started out in 2005 working with a local driving school on a franchised basis, before going it alone for several years. In 2010 I established my own driving school, Drive Ahead School of Motoring, which now offers franchises to other driving instructors. I'll share my experiences with you, and give you an insight into how my experience can help your business succeed.

Over the years I've had some great successes. I have also made mistakes in business and have not always made the right decisions. As a new instructor I often found it hard to get the right business information. I'm sharing my knowledge with you now so you can avoid making the same mistakes I did, and can hit the ground running. Some sections of this book can be actioned very quickly, other items you may want to put on a roadmap to revisit later on.

There are many great aspects to being a driving instructor. You'll meet learners from a wide range of backgrounds with all sorts of dreams and ambitions. You'll be with them as they grow in confidence and ability, from their first gear change through to the elation of passing their driving test and beyond. Knowing you've helped them gain that freedom is a huge positive.

However, there's also lots of things you need to consider as a business owner, which is what I'm going to help you to understand in this book. In 2019 I took the decision to train as a bookkeeper. After qualifying to Level 3 in Bookkeeping and Accounting and Level 4 in Self-Assessment Tax Returns with the Institute of Certified Bookkeepers, I gained my practice licence, and in 2020 I set up Drive Ahead Bookkeeping. I'll be using this knowledge, along with my experience of running a successful driving school, to help you become better at business. Each chapter highlights a different area of your business that you need to consider:

- Getting started – how are you going to set your business up? What options are there in financing a car and what impact do they have on your tax bill?
- Marketing – how are you going to attract new clients to your business?
- Finances – what records do you need to keep and how do you keep them? What expenses

are you able to claim for? What financial planning do you need to do?

- Outsourcing – Are you able to offer everything your learner needs, or do you need to bring in help from elsewhere?
- Health and Wellbeing – What impact can being a driving instructor have on your health and wellbeing?

Whatever your experience, I will help you to understand the action you need to take to improve your business!

This book doesn't need to be read from cover to cover. You may already be an established instructor and not want to read through the getting started section and that's absolutely fine. Just find your own starting point and work through as you see fit. However, I'm sure even the most experienced instructors can find something to take away from every chapter. One thing I do ask of you though, is to TAKE ACTION NOW! So many people are guilty of reading books or going to events and coming away feeling really positive about their future, but then do absolutely nothing about it. Then in a few years' time, they wonder why nothing has improved about their business or their financial situation. Please take the information and do something with it, that's all I ask.

Throughout the book you will see the images below when there's resources available for you to download. Simply type the address into your web browser or scan the QR code with your phone to access our Link Tree page. From there you'll be able to access all of the downloads.

WWW.LINKTR.EE/DRIVEAHEADBOOK

As you're getting through the book, please get in touch with me on social media. The links to my social channels are also available using the download links above. I'm happy to answer any questions you may have and I'd love to hear your feedback from the book.

PART 1

GETTING STARTED

After you qualify, there are a number of important decisions to make before you actually start working as a driving instructor. By the end of this chapter, you will learn what actions you need to take. There may be areas where you need to do a little more research, but this section will equip you with the foundations to get your business off the ground. As you read through the chapter, tick off each item from the list below when you've made your decision as to whether each will apply or you have already completed the task:

- o Are you going to work with an established driving school on a franchise basis or are you going to work independently from the start?
- o What car will you use for your lessons? How will you finance it? (This is very important to

consider and will have implications on your
tax bill, but again, I'll go into that more later)
o Who will provide your insurance?
o How much will you charge for lessons?
o You need to register as self employed
o Will you be a sole trader or will you set up a
limited company?
o Do you need to register for VAT?
o How will you manage your diary?
o How will you track your income and
expenditure?
o Who is going to do your books?
o You need to set up a bank account for your
business (not necessarily a business bank
account though, I'll explain later)
o How will you accept payment?
Cash/Card/Bank Transfer
o Do you have terms and conditions including a
cancellation policy?
o Do you have finances in place if you can't
work for any reason?

Franchise Vs Independent

Once you've qualified as a driving instructor, one of
your initial decisions needs to be are you going to
join another driving school or are you going to go it
alone? Pretty much every single driving instructor is
self-employed, which means you run your own
business. I'll explain more about that in the finance

chapter.

Your first years in any business are your formative years, and statistically a lot of businesses (not specifically driving schools) fail during this period. Therefore, it's important you thoroughly consider these options carefully.

What is a franchise?

A franchise is an agreement between yourself and another driving school to use their brand and processes to run your own business. If you've ever seen one of the national driving schools, Red, Bill Plant, AA etc, all of their driving instructors are franchisees for that school. A fee is paid to the school, anything from around £50 a week to £250+ a week, and in return they will provide you with some or all of the following:

A supply of pupils

It goes without saying, if you don't have any learners in your car, you can't make any money and will soon be out of business! The supply of pupils is without doubt your biggest challenge as a driving instructor, especially in the early days. You may be fortunate to have a 17-year-old son or daughter who has lots of mates who want to learn how to drive. But what happens next year when they've all passed their test?

Where will your supply come from? Over time you will start to get recommendations from past pupils, and as the years progress this can be quite a substantial amount. However, they can be very sporadic. You often get no recommendations for months on end, then suddenly 5 or 6 may come through in one go. That doesn't always coincide with the spaces that appear in your diary.

So what's your plan for marketing in those 'dry' periods? There are a number of ways to market yourself if you decide to go independent, though they can often be very time consuming to do and/or very expensive if not done correctly. Have a read through the Marketing chapter to get some ideas before you make a final decision. Some people have no interest in doing their own marketing, and therefore the additional cost of a franchise is outweighed by the time it frees up to do other things.

An established driving school should have various marketing methods in place to bring in learners and should be aware of their instructors' needs to provide a regular supply of new pupils.

Use of the driving schools branding – roof box, vehicle graphics, stationery (business cards etc)

When you join a franchise, for someone outside the business looking in, it will appear as you are part of the same company. Your car could have their graphics on it or a roof box on top. Your stationery (business cards etc) will bear the company name, and 'Joe Public' will probably assume you're employed by the company. The benefit of this can be that people recognise brands and may be more likely to choose a known driving school compared to an unrecognised individual instructor who they may not know. However, if there are poor instructors also in the franchise, they can damage the reputation of the school and have a negative impact on the other instructors' individual reputations. If you were to go independent, you may just use your own name or you may come up with your driving school name. A roof box with a basic design can be bought for approximately £100. If you decided to create your own logo and brand then the costs can be significantly more if you need to have images professionally designed.

Use of Theory Test software for your pupils to use

Many instructors and driving schools offer access to

apps and websites for their learners to study for their theory test. As an independent you can subscribe to a 'solo' account, whereas a franchise may include the access as part of the fee. It's not a huge cost, but it is another thing to consider if you're working out costs when going independent.

Ongoing continuous professional development (CPD)

Once you've qualified as an instructor it's really important to keep developing your skills as both an instructor and a business owner. Surprisingly, very few instructors take any extra training after they qualify. You often see instructors leave the profession when the DVSA (Driving and Vehicle Standards Agency) make changes to the test or to the way they expect lessons to be delivered. This is often due to their unwillingness to progress and develop themselves. Every few years you will be assessed by the DVSA on your continued ability to teach (The Standards Check). Some driving schools will offer CPD either for free or at a reduced cost.

The use of a car

If you join a national franchise (some local franchises offer this too, but not many), then they may offer a car as part of their package. This will be matched by an increase in the franchise fees. This may suit you if you want the convenience of a 'one stop shop' where everything you need is there, or if you're not in a financial position to be able to get finance on a car directly yourself.

If you decide to use your own car, there are a number of options to think about. From using a car you already own, to purchasing a new one to having a lease car, there's a lot to consider. I give a full breakdown of your options in the finance section of the book.

Accounting support

Many driving instructors don't see themselves as running a small business and therefore don't keep adequate records or understand the financial side of their business properly. I go into this in a lot more detail in the finances section of the book. Some driving schools may offer accounting support as part of their franchise. It may just be in the form of record keeping, or it could be a full package that includes full accounting and tax return support.

Uniform

Some franchises will provide branded clothing for you. This may include items such as polo shirts, sweatshirts or a maybe a coat.

Diary Management

Most franchises will include some form of diary management. Many have apps that can be installed on your phone or tablet and connect to an online diary which can also be accessed by the school. This means the school can see a live version of your diary and book in new learners in your available spaces.

Ongoing support

If things go wrong then you should have support from the franchise. You may have performed poorly on a standards check, or you may be having issues on lessons. Whatever the case, there should be a point of contact from your franchise provider that can assist you and give you any necessary guidance.

Duration of the franchise

If you decide a franchise is for you, then before you sign the contract, make sure you check all of the terms and conditions, especially the length of the contract. Personally, I only require a 2-week notice period for my instructors to leave. I don't believe in tying people into long contracts, and I'm confident enough in the service I provide that my instructors will be happy. Some schools, especially the national ones, have very lengthy contracts, with some tie-ins lasting up to 2 years. This is a long commitment and can provide very costly!

Hopefully, that's given you a better understanding of your options as you start this exciting journey. I'm sure it's also raised more questions to consider that you'd not thought of previously. I'll expand on these ideas throughout the rest of the chapter.

Joining an Association

There are several national associations and many local associations that you may decide to join.

There are many national associations including:

- Driving Instructors Association (DIA – www.driving.org)
- ADI National Joint Council (ADINJC – www.adinjc.org.uk)
- Motor Schools Association (MSA – www.msagb.com)
- The Association of Approved Driving Instructors (AADI – the aadi.co.uk)
- The ADI Federation (adifederation.org)

These associations give support to the driving instructor industry and provide training courses and learning materials as well providing Professional Indemnity and Public Liability Insurance. The DIA, ADINJC and the MSA have also come together to create the National Associations Strategic Partnership (NASP – www.n-a-s-p.co.uk). They work together to focus on protecting and promoting the interests of the driving instructor industry.

Another group that covers the UK is the Driving Instructor and Training Collective (DITC – www.theditc.co.uk). The Driving Instructor and Trainers Collective (DITC) was formed off the back of COVID, as it recognised the lack of a 'macro industry'. As an ADI or interested in becoming one trustworthy information can be hard to find. As a pre-PDI it is wrapped in sales patter, or bare requirements from the DVSA. Finding tools and resources is challenging and, we hate to say it, many are behind the times. The Collective aims to tackle this with a growing website plus a (tax deductible) subscription membership providing discounts and saving to members.

If you are looking for national or local associations or options the DITC is a great resource to start with. There are also many local associations present to offer support to their region. Being a driving instructor can feel like an isolated job sometimes, so it's good to get to local meetings and get to know other instructors from your area. These associations often have dealings with local DVSA officials and examiners, so it can be a good place to raise any concerns or have questions answered about local testing.

Choosing a Car

If you've decided to join a franchise that doesn't provide a car, or you've decided to go it alone and become independent, then you need to give serious consideration as to your choice of car. From the make and model of your car to the way you finance it, there's a lot to think about. Below I'll go through the key points to help you understand your options.

Make and Model

Your car is your office and is also your shop window. Driving past the local college in a 15-year-old banger isn't the greatest selling tool. On the flip side of that, the latest GTi model of your favourite car might turn heads, but is the appearance of the car going to generate enough income to make it worthwhile?

It's about finding a balance of looks, comfort and affordability.

Many learners like to learn in a smaller car such as a Corsa or a Fiesta as they believe they couldn't drive anything bigger. I know many instructors who have had quite large cars though and their learners just adapt to the size, it isn't really an issue.

Comfort

You need to make sure you're comfortable in the car, so whatever you choose, make sure you spend at least a couple of hours in it and ask around for other instructors' opinions. Once you've chosen your car it's going to be at least a year or two before you can change again without incurring substantial costs, so it's important you choose the right one. Driving instructors are prone to deteriorating health (especially lower back pain – see the health and wellbeing section for more on this) so an uncomfortable seat is the last you thing you need.

New or Used?

Having a new car is nice. Over my 15 years as an instructor, most of my cars have been from new. The downside of a new car is that they lose value very quickly. It's quite common to lose 30-40% of the value of the car in the first year. Therefore, if you do buy new, it is generally financially better to keep the car for a few years for the costs to even out. On the plus side, a new car gets a warranty and you get some piece of mind that if things go wrong early on then it's covered. Be careful on the terms of the warranty though. As driving instructors often do high mileage (it's not uncommon to do 30,000 miles a year) then the warranty would go off the mileage allowance. So, for example, a 5-year, 60,000-mile warranty would actually only cover you for 2 years.

There can be lots of really good used cars available. Generally, you need to keep an eye out for one's with low mileage and that have a decent warranty still attached to them. I've seen instructors that, with the right care and regular servicing, have managed to keep a car running for 10 years or more!

Finance

In the finance section of the book, I go into a lot more depth about how the way you finance your car will affect your tax bill. I must highlight that I am not a financial adviser and cannot give you specific advice on finance. Below is a brief summary of the finance options generally available to you, it is your decision as to which option you choose. If you're unsure then please get some professional advice before you purchase:

- Hire Purchase (HP) – With this method, you would normally put down a deposit and then the remaining cost of the car is spread out (often with interest added) over a period of time, usually 3-5 years. The bigger your deposit, the less the monthly costs will be. With HP you own the car from the start and at the end of the payment term it is yours to keep with no further payments needed. E.g. Car Value = £15000. Pay £3000 deposit, then spread the remaining £12000 over 48 months (4 years) to make a monthly payment of £250. Once the final payment is made, the car is completely yours to either keep or to part exchange. This example doesn't include any interest charges.

- Personal Contract Purchases (PCP) - Over recent years, the rise in PCP's, have made cars which previously weren't affordable now an interesting prospect for driving instructors. My last 3 tuition cars were 2 Audi A1's and most recently a fully Electric Mini. I've taken each of these on PCP agreements which has meant the monthly payments are much lower than using HP. You may need a deposit, and as before, the bigger your deposit, the lower your monthly payments will be. The garage will determine what they think the car will be worth at the end of the term (based on your expected mileage) and will set that value as a final 'bubble' payment which is due at the end of the term. As most driving instructors tend to change their cars every couple of years, it's likely you'll never reach the end of the term and make the final payment. One important thing to note with a PCP agreement is that it is based on mileage. If you underestimate how many miles you are going to do per year, then you could end up with a hefty bill at the end of the agreement. A charge is made for every mile over the limit you go.

E.g. Car value = £15000. Pay £3000 deposit. The garage determines the final value after 4 years will be £3600. So, 12,000 (car value after deposit) – 3600 (final value) = £8400 to finance = £175 a month for 48 months. At the end of the 48 months, you have the option of paying the £3600 to own the car outright, or you can give the car back to the garage and pay nothing more.

So, as you can see, the monthly payments are less than HP, but you have to make the final payment at the end to remain as the owner of the vehicle. Again, this example does not include interest charges, and is not a real quotation, it is just for illustration.

- Lease – there are numerous leasing companies that are set up specifically for driving instructors. They will provide you with a car that is fitted with dual controls, and they will provide you with all routine services and maintenance that are due over the lifetime of the agreement. A lease is more expensive than the above options, but it does give you peace of mind that if anything goes wrong with the car the lease company will take care of it.

As I stated earlier, the purpose of the above information is to give you a little guidance as to the options available when choosing a car. It's important to explore all of the options to see which is the best match for you and your individual situation. If you are unsure about the finance options, then please seek some professional guidance before you commit to a contract, as making the wrong choice can prove expensive. Also, don't forget to check out the finance section for more information about how each of these options will affect your tax bill.

Insurance

Car Insurance

It goes without saying that you will require car insurance. Standard insurance will not cover you; it needs to be driving instructor specific. There are many providers out there who can be found with a simple Google search or, if you join some of the driving instructor Facebook groups, there are often discussions about insurance providers there. Your first year's insurance, depending on postcode, and whether you're under 25 or not, can be very expensive. Going forwards though, driving instructor insurance isn't massively more expensive than regular insurance, but shop around for the best price as initial quotes tend to be very high.

Public Liability and Professional Indemnity Insurance

These policies aren't mandatory, but they are definitely recommended. Public liability insurance will cover you for things like opening your door and hitting a cyclist, or closing the bonnet of the car and your pupils' hand, causing injury. Professional Indemnity insurance covers you against claims made against you in respect of your legal liability for losses arising from a breach of professional duty.
Examples of this could include you losing data relating to your learners, or a claim arising from you breaching your terms as a driving instructor.

Hopefully neither of these policies will ever be called upon. However, it's good to have peace of mind. The policies are generally quite cheap and are actually included as part of the membership of some of the national instructor associations.

The Driving Instructor and Trainer Collective (theditc.co.uk) has an extensive resource section which goes into much more detail about insurance products and providers.

Setting up your business for tax purposes

Sole Trader vs Limited Company

When you set up your business you will need to decide whether to set up as a sole trader or a limited company. The vast majority of driving instructors will set up as a sole trader. What this means is that you run your own business as an individual and you are self-employed. The following is a description of being a sole trader from www.gov.uk/set-up-sole-trader

"You can keep all your business's profits after you've paid tax on them. You're personally responsible for any losses your business makes. You must also follow certain rules on running and naming your business."

There are a small minority of instructors who set up their business as a limited company. Being a limited company means the business is liable for any losses and not you as an individual. There are some tax savings to be made, but unless your profits (not turnover) are over approximately £40,000 or more, then the savings will be minimal compared to the increased accountancy costs incurred. These costs are due to the additional reporting that is legally required for a limited company. If you think your earnings are around this amount then it may be worth a chat with a bookkeeper or accountant.

What do I need to do next as a sole trader?

Registering for self-assessment

Self-employed people need to register with HMRC to pay tax. If you didn't send a tax return last year then you'll need to register for self-assessment and Class 2 national insurance. You can do this online and it's quite a simple process, head to www.gov.uk and search for 'register for self-assessment' for the latest information.

If you're registering for the first time then it must be done, at the very latest, by 5th October after the end of the tax year during which you became self-employed. The tax year runs from the 6th April to the 5th April the following year. So, for example, if you set up your business in July 2020, then you'd need to have registered by the 5th October 2021.

Naming your business

As a sole trader you can use your own name or you may choose a different name for your business. You do not need to register your name. Whatever name you choose must be used on all official paperwork such as invoices or letters.

If you're not using your own name, there are number of things you need to be aware of:

- You must not use a name that is already trademarked
- Your name must not be offensive
- Your name must not suggest you are connected with the government or local authority
- Your name must not make you appear as something other than a sole trader such as 'limited' or 'plc'

What about VAT?

You only need to register for VAT if your turnover goes over £85,000 in any 12-month period. As an individual instructor you will not fall into this category. It would mean that you'd need to add 20% to your lesson prices which would make you uncompetitive compared to other instructors. The additional 20% would become a liability to be paid to HMRC. However, if you decide that your want to focus on fleet training then voluntarily registering for VAT may be a good option for you. Charging VAT to another VAT registered business isn't an issue to them as it will reduce their own tax liability. For you it would mean you could claim back the VAT from your own expenses such as fuel and car expenses. If you think this may be an option for you, then please speak to a bookkeeper or accountant for further advice.

Banking

When you start your own business, you should open a separate bank account to deal with your business transactions. This makes it easy to track what income and expenditure goes through your business and will make record keeping more straight forward. Contrary to popular belief you do not need a business bank account. Just a separate personal account is sufficient. Your bank may advise you to open a business account but it's not necessary, they just want to profit from the additional fees that they will charge. This is entirely a personal decision though, and you may find the package your bank offers for business accounts may be what you're looking for. Take a look at your options and do what's best for you.

Record Keeping

It is a legal requirement for you to keep accurate records of your business transactions. Below are some recommendations of the records you need to keep:

- Details of all income including the source of the income e.g., lesson income
- A record of all expenditure. You need to have evidence of what you've spent – receipts, invoices, emails etc
- Details of large purchases such as a car
- If you're going to use your car for a mixture of personal and business use then you need to keep a log of what mileage you do for each. You can only claim fuel and motoring costs for what you use for your business. I'll go into this in more detail in the finance section but, as a rough example, if your motoring costs for the year totalled £5000 and your car use was 80% business and 20% personal, then only 80% of the £5000 = £4000 can be claimed as an expense for your business. This also applies to any item you use for a mix of personal/business use such as a mobile phone

What expenses can you claim for?

There's no definitive list as to what you can claim for, but here's a list of the most common items a driving instructor may claim for:

- Fuel
- Car Maintenance (repairs, tyres etc)
- Car wash
- Mobile phone
- Stationery (business cards, printing)
- Postage costs
- Website and related costs (hosting providers, website design etc)
- Advertising costs
- Training costs (you can claim costs for continuous professional development, but not your initial costs to train to become an instructor)
- Branded Uniform
- Business Technology and Software
- Bank charges or interest on loans/overdrafts
- Credit card charges
- Parking charges and tolls
- Franchise fees
- Accountancy/bookkeeping charges

This list is not an exhaustive list. The rule for whether something is allowed as an expense is, is it wholly, exclusive and necessary for the business? If you have any doubt as to whether it's allowable then just keep the record anyway and your bookkeeper or accountant will clarify it for you.

How do I keep the records?

The more detailed your records, the easier it is to collate all of the information at the end of the year ready for your tax return. The best way to record everything is by using cloud-based accounting software such as Xero or QuickBooks (there are many alternatives, these are just 2 common examples) or specific software tailored to driving instructors such as My Drive Time. The software will normally have an app that you can use on your mobile phone and will often have a function where you can take a photo of your receipt and enter the details of the transaction and it gets saved within the app. You can also link your bank account to the app as well so that all of your transactions appear in there automatically. Although the software companies will have you believe you just put everything in there, click a button and your self-assessment return is ready, the reality is very different. They don't take into account capital allowances (more of those in the finance section) and won't check for you if you've claimed for everything you possibly can. That is where a bookkeeper or accountant has the knowledge and experience to make sure everything is claimed for.

At the moment, online record keeping isn't mandatory, although it is estimated that in around 2023, Making Tax Digital will become compulsory for all businesses, with tax returns having to be completed quarterly rather than annually.

Although paper-based records are still acceptable, they will take longer for a bookkeeper to go through and will cost you more in the long run. As a bookkeeper, it's not uncommon for a client to bring me a bag of receipts to sort through. I'm quite happy to sift through them and record them correctly, but it is very time consuming. Basically, the more preparation you can do, the smaller the job for your bookkeeper, and the less they will charge you!

PART 2

A BUSINESS PLAN

A well-known training adage worthy of note states that "failing to prepare is preparing to fail!", sadly this is often the reason why many business ventures are not successful.

Everybody that goes into business has their own reasons for doing so. But what do you want to get out of your business? Here's a couple of things you may have considered:

- I want to be my own boss
- I want the freedom of working for myself
- I want flexible working hours
- I want to earn more money
- I want to become financially stable
- I want the pride of building my own successful business

- I want to choose who works for me

I'm sure you have numerous other reasons, but what you want, and what you end up with, can be a totally different thing if you don't have a plan. If you don't have goals, how do you know how successful your business is?

In years gone by, a business plan would've been put together to present to a bank manager when looking for funding. It would be pages and pages of detail about how your business will grow over the next few years. You would have spent days writing it, shown it to the bank manager who would only skim over it, then it'd be filed away never to be seen again – what's the point of that?

The good news is I'm not going to ask you to do that. I'm going to help you to put together your business plan for the next 3 years using an easy-to-understand concept. It'll be a live document that you will come back to time and time again to track your progress. It will evolve and change as time goes by, but you must promise me one thing – you must use it!

Your business, like life itself, will never go the way we want it to all of the time. Imagine it like a car journey. You have your destination programmed into the sat nav, and you've seen the route you're going to take. An hour into the journey, the road is blocked because of an accident. You need to make changes to your plan to reach the destination. After half an hour of detours you get back on track, but because of the longer journey you need to stop at the services to top up on fuel. You reach your destination, but it wasn't as straightforward as you expected.

You may put together what seems like the perfect plan for your business. But things will happen that mean you need to change course and find another route to get to where you want to be. The good news for you is that the information in this chapter is going to give you an easy-to-follow guide to creating your business plan for the next 3 years and how to keep it adaptable so you can cope with change.

SMART Goals

The concept of smart goals has been around for years. There have been other concepts that have come and gone, but I still believe this is one of the best and simplest methods to understand. Every goal you set yourself needs to be S-M-A-R-T:

Specific – Your goal needs to be very specific.

What do you want to accomplish? Why do you want to accomplish it? What's needed to reach the goal? You need to use strong 'action verbs' to describe your goal such as develop, conduct, build, plan, or execute.

Measurable – How will you know when you've reached your goal? Certain tasks are easier to measure than others. Financial goals for example, are easy. You'll know from your accounts (if they're kept properly – see more in the finance section) when you've reached your target. If you're goal is to work one day less per week, again, you'll know from your diary when you've achieved that. If you can't measure your progress, how do you know when you've achieved your goal?

Achievable – There's absolutely no point in setting goals that you can't achieve. Maybe your goal is to want to run your own driving school with multiple instructors. So how many instructors will you take on in your first year? Setting goals that we can't achieve is demoralising and will hinder your long-term progress. Creating goals that are achievable will give you confidence to set more goals, and receive a massive sense of achievement every time you complete them.

Relevant – Are your goals relevant to what you do?

Will it improve your business in some way? Later in the chapter I talk about 'will it make the boat go faster'. This point emphasises the importance of choosing relevant tasks in your daily life. You may realise after reading this section, that some of the goals you've set yourself aren't as relevant as you thought. As I said before though, your goals are a constantly changing piece of work, and it's absolutely ok to change them if that's the best action for you and your business.

Time Specific – How long is going to take to achieve your goal? I am going to ask you to set goals 3 years in the future as well goals for the next 7 days. For the longer tasks, break them down into smaller, easier to manage goals. You can then set a time limit for each task.

The 3 Year Plan

Before you read any further, either download and print this guide (follow the link below and select "Download your business plan templates here" or grab yourself a pen and 5 pieces of paper. At the top of each piece of paper I want you to write down each of the following (a different one on each sheet):

7 days

30 days

90 days

1 year

3 years

WWW.LINKTR.EE/DRIVEAHEADBOOK

If you're newly qualified or still going through the training process, then at the moment I would guess you're only looking ahead to the next couple of weeks and months, but I want you to start this process by looking ahead 3 years from now. Grab your piece of paper with the 3 years heading and write down where you see yourself in 3 years' time, close your eyes if it helps. Visualise what your perfect future looks like – maybe you want to have a multi-car driving school and be earning £75,000, have a nice holiday and pay off your mortgage. Maybe you want to be working less hours, or it could be you want to retire by then. It could be something to do with your house, or maybe you want to treat your children to something they've always wanted. There's no limit to this list, and no right or wrongs. This is about YOU! Everyone has different ambitions and everyone is at a different stage of life with their own priorities.

Take a good look at your 3-year plan - really take in the details – are they all SMART goals? If not, have another think about those goals and make sure they are SMART. The next thing we need to consider is how are you going to get those results? At each stage you'll dig deeper and deeper, getting into finer details. Let me give you an example - I'm going to keep the example pretty broad here and use rough figures. It is up to you to figure out the details specific to you. Let's say you want to have a multi-instructor driving school and have a turnover of £75,000 in 3 years' time (If you're not sure about the difference between turnover and profit then I explain the difference in detail in the finance section). As a full-time instructor, you may be bringing in a turnover of £40,000. This means that you need to be bringing in £35,000 from the other instructors in your business. You'll do this by creating a franchise offering (which will be fine-tuned later down the line). A typical franchise may be between £50-£100 a week without a car. At the moment we're only broadly looking at what's needed, so let's take the mid ground of £75. Allowing 4 weeks franchise holiday a year, 48 weeks x £75 = £3,600. So, to make the £35,000 target, you'd require 10 instructors (10 x £3,600 = £36,000).

1 year plan

This is where we start breaking things down a little more to provide a shorter-term plan. Take a look again at everything you put on your 3-year plan. Now, taking the example above, your aim is to have 10 instructors in your business in 3 years' time. How many will you need by the end of year 1 to make that achievable? Maybe 1 or 2? You may be really ambitious and want to set a bigger target, or you may decide that you want to leave the franchise until year 2, that's entirely your choice.

If we take a look at some other examples. Most tend to have some financial outcomes surrounding them, such as a holiday, or paying off a debt. If you want to raise £15,000 for a luxury holiday or do a large house project, then you can split that evenly as a target of £5,000 a year. Or you may have plans to grow your business over the years and may set your targets as £2000 for year 1, £5000 for year 2, and £8000 for year 3. The choice is yours. The important thing is to have it written down and have something to refer back to which will remind you of your goals.

90-day plan

3 years might have seemed a long way ahead when you started these plans. We're getting down to the nitty-gritty details of your planning now! Again, continuing the examples above, you've decided you want to have 1-2 instructors working with you by the end of the year. If you're new to teaching, then it's unlikely you'll be ready to take on instructors in your first 90 days, but it's a good idea to plan for it. What will your franchise offer look like? How are you going to market it? By the end of 90 days, you'll

want to have a clear picture in your head as to your next steps.

A target you may set yourself is to have a waiting list of learners by 90 days!

At the time of writing, my 90-day goal is to have this book published and have sales channels in place to promote it.

30-day plan

Remember, you're heading for a waiting list within 90 days, so what steps do you need to take now? What marketing methods will you use? How will you keep track of the people on your waiting list?

Your goal for your 30-day plan might be to have a full diary. This will be addressed in your 7-day plan.

As I'm writing this, part of my 30-day plan is to finish writing this book and to consider how I'm going to get it published!

7-day plan

What do you need to do to get a full diary in 30 days? What marketing are you going to use – social media, paid advertising, shop adverts, word of mouth? (see the marketing section for more ideas) Who are you going to target with your marketing?

Could you offer an incentive to your existing learners to invite their friends and family to have lessons?

My 7-day target at the time of writing is to finish this chapter.

Review It – Review It – And Review It Some More!

Your plan needs to be a continuing set of documents. Your 7-day plan needs to be reviewed every week. Personally, I like to do this on a Friday afternoon. I take a look at what I've achieved (and importantly didn't achieve!) in the current week. I then think about what went well to help me reach those results, and what I could have done differently to achieve the ones I missed. I then look ahead to my most recent 30-day plan and combine the results to create my next 7-day plan. At this point, you may also see some changes you want to make for your 30-day plan or you may decide to leave it for another week. Remember, at every step of the way, make your objectives SMART!!!

I'd personally recommend reviews as follows, but you can do them at any time as you see necessary:

7 days – weekly (it's a good idea to set yourself a time each week when you'll do the review and

commit to it)

30 days – 2-4 weeks

90 days – every 30 days

1 year plan – between 3-6 months (although can be more frequent if needed)

3-year plan – at least annually

Pricing

Part of your business planning is to figure out how much you're going to charge for lessons. Before I go into this section further, I have one thing to say –

DON'T GIVE DISCOUNTS - EVER!!!

By this, I don't mean a block booking discount, or maybe a first lesson introductory rate. I mean "mates' rates"! It's so easy to fall into the trap of giving family and friends a big discount, don't do it. There's a number of reasons why not:

- They won't value what you do – if you charge them your normal rate, they will respect what you have to offer.

- You will feel negative going into the lesson knowing that you're not earning your full potential
- They'll tell their mates who will also want a discount. The more it goes on, the harder it is to say no
- Imagine you take a mate for driving lessons and deduct £5 per lesson for them. £5 isn't a great deal of money, right? They then take 40 hours of tuition from you. You've now lost out on £200 of income. A few months later their son comes along who also wants the same discount – we're now up to £400 in lost income and the cycle keeps going – I'm sure you've got the picture by now!

As an owner of a driving school franchise, I've always believed in trying to provide the best for the instructors that work with me. That includes having someone always on hand to answer calls, online and mobile app booking systems, accounting support – but something very important to me (and I'm sure to them too) is to provide them with a rewarding lesson rate.

Driving instructors are all business owners. The purpose of a business it to make money – it's a simple definition, but in essence that's it! It's unbelievable how many driving instructors you speak to who are massively undercharging for their work and seem quite happy about it!

For the past couple of years, my driving school has charged £35 an hour for automatic lessons. Now, on the face of it, it looks like a high figure, and many learners say to me "oh you must be minted getting £35 an hour!". Now don't get me wrong, I've made a good income from being a driving instructor for a number of years now, and have certainly come a long way from £19 an hour when I started back in 2005. What many people don't look at though is the costs incurred by driving instructors, but this is what you must do to ensure you remain profitable and earning the income you want.

Adding Value

All driving instructors offer driving lessons. But what can you do to make yourself stand out from everyone else? Some ideas you could consider are:

- Theory test support (you can subscribe to software that your learners can access)
- Have resources that your learners can use. These could be physical things such as handouts, or it may be a selection of 'how-to' videos on YouTube

- Look to further yourself by gaining additional qualifications. The part 3 is only the start of your instructor development, it's important you keep looking to better yourself throughout your career.

So how much should you charge?

To begin with I want you to make a list of the following outgoings your business has to make for 1 year (when you've finished this section, keep these figures safe as we'll use them again later in the book):

- The yearly cost of your car
- Fuel costs
- Insurance costs
- Franchise fees
- Breakdown cover
- Membership of a professional body (DIA, ADINJC etc)
- Mobile phone costs
- Website costs
- Advertising costs
- Accountancy / Bookkeeping fees
- Any other expenses your business may incur – think about every possible item you can.

Then think of how many weeks holiday do you want throughout the year? For this example, let's say 4. Take 4 from 52 weeks of the year to leave 48 weeks where you can earn. Add up all of the costs you've written down above, I've got a very broad example here:

- The yearly cost of your car (£3,600)
- Fuel costs (£3,500)
- Insurance costs (£500)
- Maintenance costs (£500)
- Franchise fees (£3,500)
- Breakdown cover (£250)
- Membership of a professional body (DIA, ADINJC etc) (£100)
- Mobile phone costs (£400)
- Website costs (£100)
- Advertising costs (£500)
- Accountancy / Bookkeeping fees (£500)
- Any other expenses your business may incur – think about every possible item you can.
- Also, don't forget to take income tax into account. I go into this in much more detail in the finance section. But if you have an amount of cash you need per year, then you need to consider all deductions and outgoings!

This example totals to £13,450.

The next part is to work out how much money you want to take home in a year. In this example, I'll use £25,000. Add the expense total that we calculated above (£13,450) to give £38,450. This is how much turnover (money coming into the business) you require to reach your goal. Now divide that by 48 (the number of weeks you want to be working) to give roughly £800 – this is the amount you need to bring in per week to reach your goal.

Your next decision is how many hours do you want to be working in a week? You need to consider that if your lessons are 1 hour long then you'll have to travel to your next lesson which is time you're not getting paid for. If you can get your pupils to take 90 minute or even 2-hour lessons then you'll make your business more profitable as there's less downtime between lessons. In this example, if we say 5 lessons per day for 5 days (I know many instructors work much more than this, this is purely an example). This gives us 25 working hours. Now divide £800 (the amount you need to make per week) by 25 (the number of hours you'll be earning) = £32. This is the minimum lesson price you need to be charging to reach your goal!

You could charge less and work more hours to make the same profit (but why would you!) – or you may decide to work more hours to make your end of year profit even higher.

Preparing for the worst

It's important to remember that not every week is the same. It's inevitable you will get lessons cancelled (although with good terms and conditions you can clamp down on these). Bad weather may stop lessons, you may get ill, there's a number of reasons you may not earn and you need to be ready for that. At the time of writing, we're a year into the Covid-19 pandemic. This is hopefully a once in a lifetime event, but I know many instructors that have gone out of business because they didn't have any contingency plans and fell through the net of government support.

A good idea that I work with is, when you can, make more money in a week than you need, but pay yourself a wage like you would in an employed job. So, if you need to earn £800 but actually made £1000, keep the extra £200 in the bank. Over time this will build up and is either there as a backup, or if it's built up significantly, you may want to take a lump sum as a bit of a bonus! I will go into this more in the cashflow section later in the book.

Review It

I know instructors who have kept the same pricing for years and years. It's important to keep reviewing your prices, I would recommend you do this, at the very minimum, on an annual basis. Car prices, fuel costs, the cost of living, house prices and much more increase on a regular basis. If you were in an employed job, you would receive a pay review and normally get a rise every 12 months. As a business owner, it is your own responsibility to look after yourself in this respect so make sure to set a date in your diary to review it!

Part 3 – Marketing

If you've decided to join a franchise then chances are you won't need to do too much marketing in the early days as your franchise provider should be providing your learners. However, it is good idea to do some marketing to get your name known and to bring in some recommendations. That's essential if you plan to go it alone later down the line.

On the other hand, if you're thinking of flying solo, unless you're fortunate enough to have kids or relatives who are old enough to want to learn to drive, and who have loads and loads of mates who also want to learn to drive, then chances are you going to need to do some marketing. But, don't panic, you don't need a marketing degree to get started!

There are so many ways you can market your

business and this is an ever-changing landscape. With constant changes to technology, and with new social media apps and trends appearing and disappearing on a regular basis, you need to constantly keep learning and adapting. Fortunately for you, as an instructor of 16 years, I've tried and tested many different methods of marketing. Some have worked – some haven't! I don't have any marketing qualifications; I'm speaking to you from experience of what works as a driving school owner.

Have a look at the infographic on the next page which shows a range of ways you can market your business. Some are very cheap to do but take a lot of time, others can be more expensive but with more instant results. We'll dig deeper over the coming pages:

Recommendations

Zoom /
Public Speaking

Blogging /
Social Media Content

Paid Social Media Ads

Mainstream Media Advertising

Time Required

Cash Expense

Size of Potential Audience

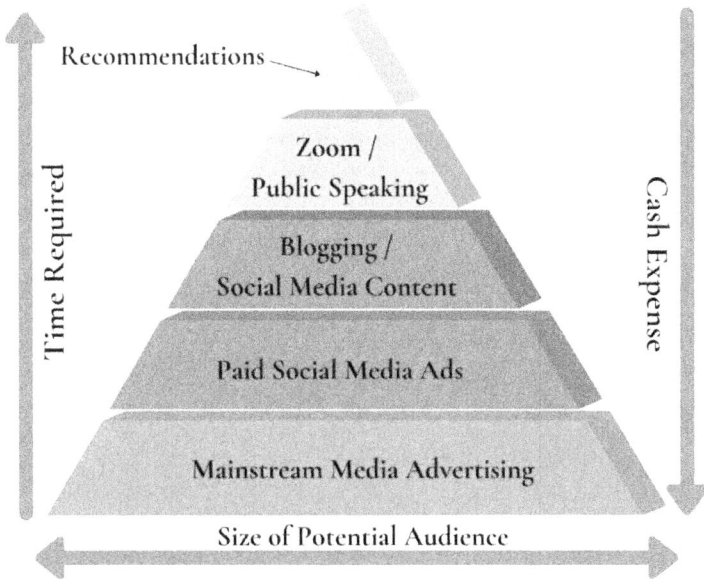

In all probability, you may well find that enquiries from the bottom of the pyramid will be asking about cost a lot more than those at the top. At the lower levels, you're promoting your business to people who have probably never heard of you and will find it hard to differentiate you from any other driving instructor. These potential customers will often be buying a service based solely on price and you don't want to be getting into a price war! – (remember your minimum lesson price from the previous chapter?)

The closer you get to the top of the pyramid, the

more likely you are to come into contact with people who know about you, they may even recognise you or your brand – they're a warm prospect! These are the people you want to be doing business with. They've already bought in to you before they've discussed price. Often with recommendations, they'll just want to book in with you, they won't even ask about the price!

One of the most important things about marketing is to not rely on one particular advertising method. As I said above, the marketing landscape is constantly changing. You may currently be getting loads and loads of recommendations which is fantastic, so you decide to cut down on your Facebook posts! But recommendations can be like a bus, you don't get any for ages, then all of sudden you are inundated with calls. So, what happens in those dry periods? Where will the work come from?

Another way to think of the various different marketing methods is as pillars. Yours business is on top, and the pillars are your foundations keeping you up. If you only had one pillar, you'd be very unsteady and could fall at any time. The more pillars you have, the stronger your foundations will be and the more stable your long-term business is.

Below we take a look at the different tiers of the pyramid and how they can be implemented into your business…

Mainstream Media Advertising

Let's start at the base of the pyramid – mainstream media advertising. At the start of your instructor journey, you're unlikely to be dipping your toe into the world of mainstream media. As the graphic shows, the potential audience here is the biggest, it doesn't take a lot of time, but it's very expensive! If you're running a school with multiple instructors, then mainstream media might be the right route for you. A local radio advert for example, could easily cost you £1000 for a week of coverage. Now the reach is huge, local radio has thousands of listeners, so has the potential to provide plenty of new learners. But if you're working on your own, what are you going to do with all of those learners??? You just wouldn't have the space and it becomes very expensive, and gives you a bad reputation if you can't take on the people you've been advertising for.

Back in 2011, a lady in Berkshire, Rachel Brown, who ran a cake shop on her own, decided to place an advert on Groupon to generate some extra business. She got great coverage, but brought in 8,500 orders. Now, a large business would be rubbing their hands together at the prospect of all of these orders. But poor Rachel who normally makes 100 cakes a month had to increase production to 102,000 cakes that month. She had to bring in 25 agency staff who worked day and night to complete the orders (which were heavily discounted). It wiped out her profit for the year, and it almost caused her business to go bust! – so for now, I'd leave the mainstream media well alone, and if and when you're big enough to warrant an advertisement on the TV or radio then seek some professional advice first.

Whenever you run a paid advert of any kind, it's hugely important to work out your return on investment (ROI). If you don't measure the cost effectiveness of an advert then you can't compare it to other forms of advertising. The way to do this is:

$$\frac{\textbf{total cost of advertising}}{\textbf{number of enquiries}} = \textbf{cost per enquiry}$$

So, if you spent £50 and got 10 enquires then £50/10 = £5 per enquiry. You then also need to consider how many of those enquiries turn into bookings. If out of the 10 bookings you only take on 1 new learner, it now becomes £50/1 = £50 per new learner, which is considerably more expensive than the figure above. By keeping track of how many enquiries you turn into bookings, you can measure how successful your selling is and the quality of the enquiries that are coming through to you. You will find that certain sources have better success rates than others and this is something you need to continue to review over time.

Paid Social Media Ads

As the graphic suggests, it's less expensive than mainstream media, it still doesn't require a great deal of time, and it has a great reach. I personally use paid social media ads quite frequently. Facebook, for example, makes it very easy to place an ad within a few minutes. You can be very specific in choosing your audience – you can choose to advertise to men or women, you can choose your age range, and you can choose what location you want to target. So maybe, your target audience is 17-year-olds in Stoke on Trent, or maybe you've found a niche market in teaching older learners and want to target your advert to 40–50-year-olds. Whatever your target is you can be very specific. Another good feature of a Facebook advert is that you can target friends of people who already like your page. This means they're already warm to your business as it will tell them that their friends also like your business. I go into more detail about the different ways of setting up Facebook for your business later in the chapter.

Before your commit to spending money on adverts though, find out what social media platform your current learners are using. Some teens are moving away from Facebook (because that's where mum and dad hang out!) and prefer to use Tik Tok or Instagram instead. If your learners aren't using a particular platform, then posting there, no matter how regularly, is just a waste of time.

As above, it's really important to keep track of your Return on Investment to see how financially successful your campaign has been.

Blogging/Social Media Content

Posting regular, useful and informative content is a great way to encourage conversation with your potential learners. It can be completely free to do, or you may decide to pay someone to post content on your behalf. It can be quite time consuming to constantly be writing and posting new content and it does take a little time to build an audience. I would recommend you plan time in your diary each week or month to write and schedule posts for the week/month ahead. It's very easy to create nice little images or memes to accompany your posts using sites such as canva.com and you don't need loads of experience to do it.

Have a good think about what your potential learners want to see – if you've found a niche market then target to that – what you want to post isn't necessarily what they want to be reading about. Every driving school in the country (including mine) is posting pictures of their students who passed their tests. It's great to see, but isn't going to differentiate you from any other school. Try and create unique and engaging content. Posting videos is a great way to encourage engagement. It may feel uncomfortable at first, I certainly wasn't a fan of making videos at the beginning, but the more you do, the easier it gets. When people are scrolling through their news feeds, they can easily swipe past a picture, but videos have a much greater response.

In addition to social media, if you can create original and interesting blogs on your website then it can help boost your website rankings. The better the quality of your posts, the more people share your posts, then the more the search engines see your relevance and will give you a boost up the rankings. This takes a while to do so you will absolutely not see the immediate effects, but be patient.

Zoom/Public Speaking

Now we're almost at the summit of the pyramid and you'll see the balance is now changing to less expense but more time intense. There can be many opportunities to speak in public, especially due to the much greater adoption of Zoom for online meetings arising from the Coronavirus pandemic.

Where you focus your time here depends on if you have a particular niche. For example, you may have a lot of experience with a particular learning need such as autism or dyspraxia, or maybe you have experience of teaching people with disabilities. There will be local groups all over the country that are there to cater for all sorts of needs. Have a look on social media to identify groups you could join. It can be nerve-wracking at first if you're not used to public speaking. But the thing to remember is – you are the expert!

Also, there are frequent opportunities to speak to local media. Whenever there's an item on the news related to learning to drive, or maybe there are proposed changes on local roads, they're always crying out for driving instructors to talk to. Most instructors shy away from it, so get in there and get yourself known as the local expert.

Recommendations

Now this is the ultimate goal and is your key to unlocking a great long-lasting business with the best earning potential. Unfortunately, recommendations don't happen overnight, and as I mentioned before, they don't always come to you on a consistent basis. So how do you get recommendations?

To bring in the best quality recommendations who are willing to pay the highest lesson fees you need to be good at what you do and provide a great experience for your learners. Below are a number of ways you can do this:

- Be on time – if you've arranged a time for a lesson, then be there on time! Yes, you will get stuck in traffic on occasions, if you do, let your learner know, don't keep them waiting. Plan your lessons to allow plenty of journey time to arrive on time. Likewise, make sure your learner gets the full time they've paid for. There's nothing worse than an instructor who is always finishing 5 minutes early. There may be an odd occasion where you have to, but be upfront at the beginning of the lesson and make sure you add the lost time onto a subsequent lesson.

- Look professional – you don't need to wear a shirt and tie. I'm not saying don't – if that's your look, then great. But don't feel like you have to. Some learners are much more comfortable if you're more casual. I personally wear jeans and a polo shirt most days - Be comfortable, but keep it smart.
- Give value to your learners – do you have handouts they may find useful? Have you created videos to help them learn on YouTube? Do you offer them theory test support? There are a lot of supplementary apps available for both iOS and Android devices now, could you offer them to your learners?
- Don't smoke in your car – for one, it's illegal. Your car is classed as a public space and is affected by the indoor smoking ban that came into place in 2007, and you have to have a no smoking sticker displayed in your car. Just as importantly, your non-smoking learners really won't appreciate a smoky car.
- Have good communication channels. In this modern age people want answers now. They expect that if they send you a message at 9.30 in the morning that they'll get an answer in an hour or two, not at 5 in the afternoon. If you struggle to find time to answer calls then consider outsourcing and getting someone to

do it for you (see the outsourcing section later on).

- Strive to be the best at what you do. You may have qualified as a driving instructor, but that must not be the end of your learning! Continuous Professional Development is essential for you to stay on top of your game. Put yourself a budget aside to spend on developing yourself. It may be to explore different teaching methods, learning about teaching learners with special educational needs or disabilities, or exploring new social media platforms to interact with your learners. There is so much you can do to better yourself – reading this book is a step in the right direction!

Don't be afraid of asking your learners to recommend you to their friends, you could even offer an incentive such as a discounted lesson for every friend they recommend. It's also good to ask for reviews from your learners. If someone visits your website or social media page, if they can see testimonials from real life learners then they're more likely to buy from you. Have a process in place for gathering reviews. A good time would be mid-way through the learning process, once you've had time to build a relationship with them. Another is just after they've passed as they'll be over the moon and most likely to leave you a 5-star review at that point.

Creating your brand

When you start your driving school, you are joining around 40,000 other small business owners offering driving lessons. Now you don't need to compete with them all, unless you're planning on creating a national driving school (which I assume you're not – well not yet anyway!). You just need to get known in your local area.

What's your identity?

The first thing to consider is, what are you going to call your driving school? Many instructors use their name, others create a business name, and there are some fantastic pun named driving schools – local to me, there's 'Bat out of L', 'L of a way to pass', and 'What the L'.

It's important to think about what your plans are for the future. If you're planning on growing your school and taking on more instructors in the longer term, then your name needs to be something that is suitable for everyone. I do know of some very successful driving schools who are based on the owner's names – Bill Plant in particular did very well for himself. But most multi-car schools use a generic name such as my own – Drive Ahead School of Motoring.

If you're struggling to find a name, have a chat with family and friends, or maybe put a post on social media asking for ideas. I had worked for a franchise when I first qualified, before going on my own after a few years. I asked people for suggestions for my driving school name, then created a shortlist and asked my learners to vote for their favourite. My wife, Becky, was made up when it was her suggestion that was chosen! Before you make a final decision though, have a search to make sure your name's not already in use. Just a simple Google search will help you with that. If you're in York and there's another school in Cornwall with the same name then it's not really an issue (as long as it's not Trademarked). There's unlikely to be any conflict of interest. However, you can't call yourself the same thing as another school in your area or surrounding areas.

Logo Design

Getting a logo designed can be a very costly part of your start up. Using a graphic design company can often cost hundreds of pounds. Now, don't get me wrong, the results you get will be amazing, and they may provide you with different versions of the logo for different uses (website – social media – print).

However, in this digital age we live in, it's never been easier or cheaper to create some fabulous looking logos. If you're feeling creative (or maybe you have family or friends that are) then you can create your own using various websites. I mentioned it earlier in the book, but canva.com is great for doing this. You can also outsource using a site such as fiverr.com which is great for finding freelancers who are willing to do the work for you. Many of the people on there are students or people that do it for a hobby, although some make a good living from their work there. Take a look at the reviews before finding someone you're happy with.

Marketing Materials

As a new business owner, it feels nice to have your own line of stationery – business card, letter heads, flyers etc. As a driving school owner though you won't have use for most of them on a regular basis. It's rare that you'll write a letter to anyone at all, though if you do, it's easy enough just to add your logo to a word document. Business cards and flyers can be created for a reasonably low cost. There are plenty of websites out there that will provide you templates to create your own designs and then print and deliver them to you.

Do I need a website?

In short, no.

In years gone by, the first thing any new business would do is to have a website built. Often businesses would spend hundreds of pounds on a website. Yes, they look good, but unless you have a lot of money to spend on it, chances are very few people will ever see it. In my local area, there are at least 250 other driving instructors. The first page of a search engine typically shows 10 results. Research shows that most people rarely go past page 1 in the search results, they certainly don't get past page 2. So, unless you're on the first page, the only way of getting your page seen is to use paid adverts which, as we've already seen above, is potentially very expensive.

I would focus your initial time creating and managing your social media accounts which I go into more details later in this section.

If you do still decide to create a website then you could spend anything from £200 to over £1000 for something professionally done. There are options to create your own such as WordPress or Wix, but they do still require some design skill and technical know-how to make a good-looking site.

You will then need to spend time thinking about what content you're going to put on the website. It's important to keep it reasonably brief. The site should be about what's in it for the learner. What can you do for them? How can you help them to get their driving licence? How are you different to other driving instructors? It's a good idea to include some testimonials on your site. Prospective learners visiting your website, don't know the difference between you or any other instructor in your area, so providing reviews from other people gives them some reason to believe in you and what you have to offer.

As I mentioned previously, everyone is competing for the first page on Google. You'll regularly receive messages from marketers claiming to be able to get you onto page 1 of Google – but guess what? They probably won't, and if they do, you won't stay there without more considerable investment. The best of way of ranking well is to create consistently good content and getting other websites to link back to yours. Writing quality blogs and becoming an expert in your field, so that people want to come back and read your posts, is one of the key elements to ranking well with the search engines.

This is all part of what is called SEO or Search Engine Optimisation. Unfortunately, the goal posts for SEO change on a regular basis, which is why I'm not going to go into more in this book. From the time it's taken for me to publish the book, and then for you to be reading it, the content I've written about SEO could already be outdated. If you do decide you want to create a website, then do your research. Find out what the latest trends are, and decide if the time and money required to do so is really going to bring you a good return on your investment.

Google My Business

Google get 92% of search traffic. In addition to creating a website, another way to get an online presence it to create a listing on Google My Business (GMB). It allows you to get access to Google map searches and organic rankings without necessarily needing a website (although engagement and clickthrough are dramatically higher if you have one). GMB allows you to create a single page site for free and is understandably Google friendly, therefore giving you some online presence, albeit limited.

YouTube

YouTube has now become the second largest search

engine in the world behind Google. If you can produce good quality training videos and How To guides then it becomes a great resource to direct your learners to. And again, by linking your YouTube channel to your website and social media pages, it will help your website climb the search rankings. With the quality of mobile phone videos and the increased presence of HD dash cams, it has never been easier to create and post videos to YouTube as well as your other social media channels.

Using social media for your website

Over the past 10 years social media has become the go to platform for getting your business out there. Each platform has its own advantages and disadvantages, and the effectiveness of each platform changes as new platforms come online. It's important to speak to your learners over time to see what social media they're using. Traditionally Facebook was always the go-to platform for driving schools to promote their business. However, teens started to become reluctant to post on Facebook because Mum and Dad also used it and would see their content, so they started to move elsewhere. That doesn't mean Facebook isn't still a good place to be. Personally, my driving school still sees a lot of enquiries come through Facebook, both from learners directly, but also from their parents. Below I give a brief explanation of how to use each platform and why it's good for your business.

Facebook

Facebook is still the behemoth of social media. It's been around since 2004 and at the time of writing they have 2.7 billion active users – that's 1/3 of the population of the world that actively uses Facebook!

It's easy to create an account, I'm pretty sure you'll already have one, but if not head to Facebook.com and follow the instructions, it's so easy. If you don't want to, you don't need to use it for personal use. There are 3 ways you can have a presence on Facebook:

Personal page – this is where you start off, and is generally where people post their holiday pictures and share funny videos of cats. It's great for your day-to-day news, but it's not the best place to market your business.

Business page – most brands will have a business page. From here, you can tell everyone about your business and link back to your website and other social media channels. As Facebook also owns Instagram, you can set-up your business page to post to both platforms. This can save you valuable time and give you a bigger audience. It's a bit of a vanity thing, but don't get caught up trying to have the most 'likes' to your page. Yeah, it feels good getting hundreds of likes, but more importantly it's the quality of likes that is important. You can invite your friends from your personal page to 'like' your business page, but are they going to buy your services? Probably not. Facebook uses algorithms to decide who to show your content to. Just because you have 500 followers doesn't mean they will all see your post. People who react (like/comment) to your content are more likely to be shown future posts. I love my Mother-in-Law, I'm very lucky to have a good one, but she likes everything I post. It's lovely, but she's never going to buy anything I'm selling. She sees every post that I put out which is nice, but that's one less potential buyer that's not seeing my post. Also – don't invite other driving instructors to like your page. I've had literally hundreds of requests from instructors to like their pages. Why? I'm not going to have driving lessons off them. I can drive already. I am also a driving instructor! You're basically sucking the life out of your page if you're inviting people that are not in your prospective audience. You want to be inviting teenage relatives and asking them to get their friends to like it. They are the people who will want driving lessons in the future!

Groups – Facebook groups are one of the biggest growing trends on Facebook right now. Groups are little bit more informal and other people can post there to. You could create a group such as 'theory test tips for learner drivers' and invite your learners to join. By posting regular content, such as theory question of the day, or by sharing YouTube hazard perception videos, you can create conversations. People who are engaged in what you do, and see you as an expert, are more likely to buy from you. It is a slow burner, and when you only have a handful of people in the group in the early days, it can be a little demoralising when you get no engagement, but consistency is key. With all social media, it's about constantly posting quality content, in time your audience will build.

Instagram

In recent years Instagram has increased in popularity, especially with the younger audience. If you've never used the platform, it's based more on pictures than text. People post photos and videos, sometimes with a short message. Here users can 'follow' you in the same way they would 'like' you on Facebook. As I mentioned previously, you can connect your Facebook and Instagram accounts so you can simultaneously post the same content to both platforms. Again, driving test passes are a common item that driving instructor's post. You need to think about how you can stand out from everybody else. Be creative with your posts, and give value in what you offer. Making posts that others will engage with will help to build your following.

TikTok

TikTok is the baby of the social media family but is rapidly gaining in popularity in the younger generation. It is a completely video-based sharing platform. Users create videos of between 15 and 60 seconds. It's very common to see trending dance routines, people doing tricks on each other or showing off skills, but it is gaining in popularity with businesses too. By posting how-to videos and helpful tips for learners, it's quite easy to build yourself a following. The only downside with TikTok is that it's a worldwide platform, and at present, you cannot choose your audience. However, you can promote your TikTok channel to your existing users from the other platforms.

Twitter

Twitter is the poor relation in the social media family. It is often used by national businesses as a customer service platform, and it's good to read updates from your favourite sports person or celebrity, but for a driving school it can be difficult to gain much exposure here. It's not a popular choice with the younger generation so you may find your posts falling on deaf ears. However, with the right posts it can start some good conversations. Possibly the best thing about Twitter for driving instructors is the access to DVSA Help. The DVSA post quote regular updates about testing and driver related topics so that alone can be worth having an account for.

LinkedIn

There are 2 common marketing strategies - B2B (business to business) and B2C (business to consumer). As a bookkeeper I would be looking at connecting with other business owners (B2B), but as a driving school I would be wanting to connect directly to the consumer (the learner). All of the above platforms are B2C, however LinkedIn is more of a B2B platform. It's unlikely any connections you make here will create any new learners, however if you're looking to deliver fleet training it can be a good platform to connect with business owners.

Outsourcing

Outsourcing can apply to marketing, but it can be done with several other parts of your business too. As you get busier and busier it does become increasingly hard to find time to perform certain tasks in your business.

With any of the processes in your business, you need to weigh up the following – is the time you're spending on a certain task well spent? Could you use the time in a way that would be more beneficial to your business or to generate more income?

Some people find it easy to create websites, or to think of marketing posts and put them out on a regular basis. Other people struggle creatively or just can't find the time to be posting regularly. Is it worth spending an hour or so per week on this, or can you pass the responsibility onto someone else? You may have a family member or friend that could help you out for a small fee, or alternatively, there are people out there who are marketing experts and will post great quality content for you on a regular basis. As discussed earlier in the section, if you are paying someone to do something, then you need to work out what your ROI (return on investment) is to ensure it makes business sense.

Other things you may want to outsource could be taking on a phone answering service or someone to run your website. I've used Driving Instructor Services for many years for my driving school (there are several other providers who I'm sure are equally as good, but I'm just speaking from my personal experience here!). They answer my driving school phone calls, manage call back requests from my website, and book in lessons either on the phone or through my website. Yes, I could do all of these things myself, but when someone calls about a lesson, I may be busy. I then need to find the time to call them back. They may not answer and we play phone tennis throughout the day. As you start to grow your business these calls get more frequent and more difficult to deal with. Your potential learners want to speak to someone now. If you don't answer, chances are they'll move on to the next driving school on the list.

As your business continues to grow you may decide to take on another instructor. You may be able to bring in instructors who are already qualified, or you may want to bring in trainee instructors. Will you have the time or expertise to do this on your own, or will you outsource to another instructor trainer? It's something to consider early on, as you need to develop relations with other trainers and make sure that they're someone you trust and can do the job properly.

It's not a weakness to ask for help and outsource, it's about identifying opportunities for growth and acknowledging when somebody could do something better or more efficiently than you. This leaves you more time to focus on what you're good at and utilising your time in the best way!

PART 4

FINANCES

Ultimately, the main purpose of running a business is to make money, we don't go to work for the fun of it! In this section I'll run through the fundamental things you need to know in order to understand the financial function of your business. Understanding your turnover, profit, and cashflow is the starting point to making more money.

"turnover is vanity, profit is sanity, cash is a reality"

The origins of this phrase are unknown and it's widely used throughout the business world, but what do those terms actually mean, and what can you do to improve the balance? The examples I'm using below use very basic figures just to show the idea behind these concepts. I've gone into more detail in other chapters.

Turnover – turnover is how much money comes into your business. So, if over the course of the year you do 30 lessons a week @ £30 for 48 weeks (you did take some time off, right?!) = £43,200. This is your turnover. In the past many driving schools have quoted these sorts of figures in their advertising to lure in new instructors. I remember back in the early 2000's when I was looking at the possibility of becoming an instructor, I was wowed with the prospect of earning £30,000+. At the time, I worked in sales and earned significantly below this level and it seemed amazing. In reality, my end of year tax returns didn't bring in anywhere close to this much in my early years.

Profit – okay, so now this figure is a much better figure for a business owner. Roughly speaking Profit = Turnover – Expenses. Expenses aren't as black and white as they seem, they aren't simply a deduction of everything you've spent, but as I said at the start, these are rough figures and I talk about allowable expenses later on.

So, a very basic profit calculation would be:

Income from Lessons:
£43,200

Expenses:

Car Rental: £3,600 (£300 a month for 12 months)

Fuel: £3,000

Car Insurance: £500

Advertising: £500

Total Expenses:
£7600

Net Profit:
£35600

Cash – As the title suggested – cash is reality. How much cash is in your hand or in your bank? In the driving instructor industry, it's rare for you to be owed money for lessons, you should have systems in place to take payment in the car, whether that's by cash, card or bank transfer. Sometimes learners (or their parents) may even pay for a block of lessons up front. Therefore, the amount of cash coming into your business should be pretty much equal to your profit.

The problem for a driving instructor comes when they don't budget their cashflow throughout the year – generally speaking, the money won't come in equally throughout the year as in a traditional employed job. Depending on your location and the demographic of your learners, you may earn more at certain times of the year. For example, you may live in a university town and the bulk of your work comes from students. What happens to your income when they all go home for the summer or the Christmas Holidays? Are your bills spread evenly across the month? Or are you left scrambling for cash when your car payment becomes due? I'll talk about all of these issues in the cash flow section in a few pages time.

How to increase your profit

Increasing your profit is, on the face of it, pretty simple. There are 2 things that you can do – increase your income, or reduce your expenses. The wider the gap is between what's coming in and what's going out, the more profitable your business will be.

When you're running a business, it's easy to get your head down and be so focused on the day-to-day tasks that you never take a step back to review things.

Let's start with pricing. If you deliver 30 lessons a week, 48 weeks of the year, raising your lesson price by just £1 will bring in almost £1500 in extra profit. Driving instructors are renowned for constantly under charging for their lessons. I discussed pricing earlier on in the book, so you should understand how to calculate your minimum operating price. If you skipped that section, head back now and read it as it is important that you fully understand the concept. In this day and age, a manual driving lesson shouldn't be any less than £30, and around £35 for automatic. You've studied hard to become an instructor, charge what you're worth. My son has drum lessons – they're £25 an hour. His drum teacher has no qualifications – he's very open about that, but he is good at what he does. He has a couple of drum kits and pays minimal rent, and the lessons run consecutively 1 after another, so has no down time between lessons as driving instructors have. He teaches people to play drums, most will never get past it being a hobby – you teach people to drive which is with them for life. It will get them job opportunities, and it gives them freedom. I don't know what his profit it is, but I'm damn sure it's more than a lot of driving instructors. So why are you not charging more for your lessons?

Now let's take a look at expenses. Be honest with yourself here; when was the last time you sat down and looked at all of your outgoings and considered if you could do anything to reduce them? Now, don't get me wrong, there may be cheaper options, and even after you review, you might decide you want to take the more expensive option. That's your personal choice and it's absolutely fine as long as you've consciously thought about it. I know for a fact that I could get a cheaper mobile phone, but I like iPhones. I had a brief fling with a Samsung, but it wasn't for me. I looked for ways of reducing the cost but decided I didn't want to make that sacrifice.

What I want you to do is make a list of everything you spend on your business. Then take a look to see if you could do anything to lessen them. Here are a few examples:

Fuel – do you use the cheapest petrol station, or do you just use whichever is closest on your journey? Could you take out a fuel card which gives you a discount on your purchases, or maybe a cash back credit card?

Car – do you need to change your car as often as you do? Could you choose a different make or model next time to save you some money? Again, you may decide that having a nice car is a priority for your business, but as long as you've made a conscious decision about that and reviewed the options available to you, then that's fine.

Mobile Phone – many people just automatically stay with the same provider once their minimum contract has finished as it's the easiest thing to do. In the last couple of years, it's become easier and easier to change networks without loads of hassle from your current provider.

Subscriptions – it's easy to take out a subscription and forget about it. It may be an instructor related one such as membership of a professional body, or it could be a magazine or something similar. Are you utilising what you're subscribed to? Could you cancel it, or could you get the same thing elsewhere for less money?

It's important to continually repeat this review. I'd recommend around quarterly to half yearly to keep on top of your expenses.

You're self-employed – what do you need to be ready for?

I'm pretty sure that at some point in your life you've been employed by someone. When you're in employment you get:

- A regular income
- Your tax and national insurance are automatically calculated and paid for you
- Holiday pay
- Sick pay
- Paid maternity/paternity leave
- A workplace pension with contributions from your employer
- Set working hours

So why the heck would you become self-employed when everything is so rosy in employment?

- You're your own boss
- You have the potential to earn more
- Set your own schedule
- Running your own business can be very rewarding!

In terms of finances, below are a number of things you need to take into consideration to be able have the same benefits you enjoyed during employment whilst enjoying the freedom of being self-employed.

Please note, I'm not a financial advisor and cannot give you specific advice on any investment areas. The purpose of this section is to give you things to consider for your business. Please seek professional advice before you commit to any savings or investment products.

Sickness and Holidays (and even a pandemic!)

You are going to have some time off, aren't you? When you're self-employed, the temptation is to plough on through when you're sick, or not take holidays as often. When you're employed it's easy to call in sick or book a bit of time off. You know the work will get done by someone else, and chances are you may even have been paid for the first couple of days off sick. When you're self-employed you feel the pressure to carry on. From a financial point of view, if you're not working, you're not earning! But you also don't want to let your customers down.

It's difficult to find someone to cover your workload if you're sick as a driving instructor. What I'd recommend is to join local driving instructor groups or associations and get to know other instructors in your area. Then, if the time comes that you can't work, you can ask for help. It's unlikely they'd be able to cover your full diary (and you don't really want that – it's difficult for an instructor to turn up for a one-off fill in lesson and do a great job!), but there's a good chance someone could help you out if you have a driving test booked in.

Financially, it's important you put some money aside for sickness and holidays. It is recommended that you have enough money saved up that you could cover all of your outgoings for 3 months. As I'm writing this, the UK is 1 year into the coronavirus pandemic. Many driving instructors have struggled over the past year even with the support from the government. Many have gone out of business and gone back to being employed. No-one in the world ever expected such a worldwide catastrophe would come along like this, so very few would have ever saved for such long-term periods of not being able to work – I know I certainly didn't! You may be fortunate enough to have savings already, I know a lot of you reading this will not have though. If you have nothing saved yet, it's hard to imagine ever having 3 months' worth of spare cash saved, but it's possible, and will take some time to put into place. Later in the section I talk about cashflow and budgeting which will go into more detail about how to save.

In addition to this, there are insurance products for the self-employed that will pay you a percentage of your wage if you're off work through illness or injury. It does give you piece of mind, but you still need to have some money put away for the short-term. A few years back I dislocated my arm from my wrist playing rugby and was off work for 6 weeks. I did have insurance but it didn't pay out until after I was back at work, and the amount it paid was only about half of what I would have earned if I'd been working. The funny side to this story was that it was a fancy-dress charity match and I ended up in A&E wearing a bright red tutu, bright red lipstick and painted on rosy cheeks!

Pensions and Investments

In recent years it has become law that all employers automatically enrol their employees into a pension scheme. Every pay day, a small percentage of your wage is deducted and put into your pension scheme. The employer also makes a contribution to your pension.

There are no such benefits when you're self-employed. It is up to you to start your own pension scheme and to pay funds into it. The current state pension pays out £179.60 a week, and is paid out when you reach state pension age. This age bracket is being reviewed regularly so it's important you keep track of when this age will be for you. For many people, £179.60 won't even come close to the income they require, so a personal pension is a must. The amount you'll need to put in to a personal pension will depend on what sort of lifestyle you want when you retire. The later in life you start a pension, the more you'll need to pay in to reach your desired amount – so it's a good idea to start early!

You may decide that a pension isn't right for you or doesn't offer the returns you're looking for. Instead, you may want to invest your money. This could be into property, stocks and shares, or numerous other investment products. I know several instructors who have a second house that they rent out now, with the plan to sell when they reach retirement age to release the capital funds.

There are various types of pensions and investments, and I can't advise you any further on the matter. It's important to take the advice of a professional financial advisor to make sure you make the right choice for your personal situation, but I hope this section has given you some food for thought.

Cashflow & Budgeting

On paper, a business can show a good turnover and appear to be profitable. However, as I mentioned at the start of the chapter, cashflow can be one of the biggest challenges a business can face. In the following section I'm going to be very open and honest with you. I've been there and experienced those issues and have struggled with the best of them to keep my finances afloat. I'll share my experiences with you, so you don't have to go through the same as I did. I will help you thrive over the coming years – sound good?

There's a phrase that describes someone struggling with cashflow – 'living hand to mouth'. This is where you're earning money, and as soon as the money arrives in your hand or your bank it is immediately spent. Does this sound familiar? I personally have experienced this in my younger days and it is an awful experience. Having to rush from a lesson to get to the bank in time to make sure today's bills are paid, but then worrying about if you will have enough to cover tomorrow's bills, and the day after's and so on. I wouldn't wish it on anyone.

Or maybe you've been in business a little while, and every January you rush your accounts to your bookkeeper or accountant, who, days before the tax deadline, tells you you have to pay a larger amount to the tax man than you were expecting. You're panicking as you haven't saved for your tax bill, and you've suddenly got to find potentially several thousand pounds in a very short space of time. You may end up having to take a loan out to cover the payment which then makes cashflow for the following year more difficult. I'll share something with you – I've been there too! It's hard to admit, but there have been times throughout my self-employed career where I've struggled. I may have been earning very well and on the surface, everything appeared calm and effortless, but underneath, just like a duck, I was paddling like hell to stay afloat!

Over many years I've learnt from this, and studied cashflow and budgeting to get a better understanding. This has helped me to make significantly better decisions, I make a regular cash flow review for both my business and personal life, and my tax bill money is now always ready on time.

Lesson Prepayments

Before we jump into how to manage your cashflow, I want to talk about lesson prepayments with you. When a learner gives you a payment in advance for their lessons, possibly several hundred pounds, you need to realised that money isn't yours yet. You haven't earned it, so don't spend it! (Under the self-assessment section later in this chapter I discuss how to account for prepayments from a tax point of view, but for now I'm talking about the day-to-day handling of them.)

It's so tempting when you've received a prepayment and you've got all of that cash burning a hole in your pocket to go out and spend it. I've had weeks where I've had several prepayments all come in and I've got over £1000 in extra money sat there looking at me! And yes, as you can tell from my previous form, I've gone out and spent it! You think it's amazing. You maybe go out and treat yourself or a loved one, and you think this self-employed malarkey is amazing! Then a week or two down the line, reality sets in. You're bringing in very little cash as you've had so many prepayments, and you've already spent them! You're now desperately struggling for the next few weeks until the prepayments end, possibly finding it hard to make ends meet. The cycle goes on and on…

Firstly, from a legal point of view, you could be liable to pay that money back at any time. Fortunately, it doesn't happen too often, but if a learner asks for their remaining money back then you may have to give it to them. It could be that they're moving away, or there's been an illness and they can't continue. It's important to have some terms and conditions about the handling of prepayments that you share with your learners. It may be the case that you offer a discounted rate for prepayment, and if that prepayment is cancelled, then the normal rate applies and you would pay them back the difference. As I said before though, the money is not yours until you've delivered the lesson and earned it.

Top Tip – Put your prepayment money to one side until you've earned it. I put mine into an easy access savings account. Then each week just take out the money that you've earned. By doing this, it evens out your cashflow and doesn't leave you open to problems if someone requests the money back.

Saving for your tax bill

You are going to save right? – for many new business owners, their first tax bill can be a massive shock to the system. When you're in employment, your employer automatically deducts your tax and national insurance contributions for you. This means whatever lands in your bank account on pay day is all yours. That's not the case for the self-employed though. A little later in this section I go into detail about what's included in your self-assessment tax return, but as a rough guide you should be saving roughly 1/3 of your profits to make sure you have enough for your bill.

How your tax bill is calculated

The amount of tax you pay is set within earning bands which is reviewed every year. In the 2021-22 tax year the bands are as follows:

Personal allowance – how much income you can earn before you start to pay income tax. No tax is charged on this amount	**£0 - £12,570**
Basic rate income tax – all income that falls into this bracket is taxed at 20%	**£12,571 - £50,270**
Higher rate income tax – all income that falls into this bracket is taxed at 40%	**£50,271 - £150,000**
Additional rate income tax – this is the highest rate and all income over this threshold is	**£150,000 upwards**

taxed at 45%

As an example, if you earned £25,000 it would be calculated as:

£25,000 - £12570 (your personal allowance) = £12,430

You will pay no tax on the first £12,570 and will be charged 20 % tax on the remaining £12,430 (£12,430 x 20% = **£2,486**)

In addition to this you will be charged a percentage for National Insurance (NI). The self-employed pay 2 classes of NI – class 2 and class 4.

Class 2 – in 2021-22 the threshold is £6,515. If your earnings are above this then you will be charged £3.05 a week (you don't pay weekly, it's added to your tax bill).

Class 4 – in 2021-22 the threshold is £9,568. All earnings above this are deducted 9%. Any earnings over £50,270 are deducted 2%.

Budgeting and Cashflow

The difference between budgeting and cashflow, is your budget is a plan which will show expected income and expenditure for the next 12-month period. The cashflow forecast details month by month, where the money is actually going to be spent or received.

Your Budget

To start this, you'll need to look at every possible expense your business will have. Hopefully, you kept these figures from the pricing section earlier on. If not, you'll need to gather together every single expense that is likely to go through your business in the next 12 months. One figure we didn't add to your pricing figure earlier on is the budget for your tax bill. You'll need to bear that in mind from the information I've just given you. Follow the link below and select "Download the budget spreadsheet here" for your downloadable budget template. This is best downloaded onto a computer or tablet that has Microsoft Excel installed.

WWW.LINKTR.EE/DRIVEAHEADBOOK

Using the template, enter all of your expenses on a monthly basis. You could print it off and write them in manually, but by using the spreadsheet it calculates everything automatically for you. I've entered headings for the majority of expenses but left a few spaces if you have something extra that you'd like to add in. The figures you used in the pricing section may now have changed as you've considered what marketing you need to do or you may have now bought a car for your business and need to add that into the equation. A budget is a rough outline of how your business will look over the coming 12 months. Some things may change. An example of this may be marketing. You might budget for a monthly spend on paid advertising, but after a few months you may be very busy or have taken on a lot of recommendations, so you decide to put a hold on them for a month or two.

Under the income section, use your lesson price that you decided on earlier and multiply that by the number of lessons you're planning to do per day. Then multiply that by the number of working days in the month. Repeat that for each month of the year, taking into account time you won't be earning. You may want 2 weeks holiday in the summer, or maybe you want to take a week or so off at Christmas, so you need to budget for that.

Don't forget to include any money that you need to put aside for your tax bill or savings into your budget.

This may be a little time consuming, but the more thorough you are, the better prepared your business will be for the future. Now you will have a full spreadsheet detailing your business' income and expenditure for the next 12 months.

Cashflow Forecast

A budget is good, but if it doesn't get used then it's absolutely pointless. A good budget needs to be combined with a cashflow forecast. This details exactly when money will come in and out of your business and is the key to survival. Ideally you want to have a cashflow forecast for the next quarter, and then review it every month to take into account any changes that may occur. Follow the link below and select "Download you cashflow forecast here":

WWW.LINKTR.EE/DRIVEAHEADBOOK

When you first complete this exercise, you will probably find the figures you used in your budget are the same as your cashflow forecast as you've only just created them. It's important to identify where there may be shortages in your cashflow, such as when you're going on holiday, so you can plan ahead for that. Rather than spending everything you earn, it's a good idea to pay yourself a wage as you would in employment. That way you have an even amount coming in throughout the year and can still pay yourself a wage when you're not working. You also need to consider what factors may affect your income, such as more cancellations on the lead up to Christmas, or your main customers may be university students and your income drops when they go home for the summer. Every business owner will have a different scenario so it's important you really consider what's right for you. If you're a new driving instructor, you may not have a clue yet as to when your peaks and troughs of earnings will happen. That's fine, don't worry. As a guide, deduct 10% off what you expect your incoming cashflow to be. This will allow for cancellations or quieter periods.

You need to review your actual cashflow on a regular basis and enter in the actual figures for the previous month so you can compare what you projected to what actually happened. The more you do this, the better your future forecasts will be as you understand the accuracy, or inaccuracy, of your figures more. If you follow the link below and select 'Watch – budget planning and cashflow forecasting' there's a short video that explains how to use the templates.

WWW.LINKTR.EE/DRIVEAHEADBOOK

Car Finance

When you purchase a car for your business the options can be very confusing. With this post, my aim is to make things clearer for you, and hopefully help you to understand how your new car purchase will affect your accounts.

Leasing

The easiest option to understand is a lease. You pay a monthly fee to basically rent the car for a set amount of time. At the end of the period, you give the car back. With a lease you can claim back 100%

of your monthly payments. You can also claim back any motoring costs such as fuel, insurance, and maintenance (although some leases include the maintenance in the price). So, as you can see, every cost can be deducted off your end of year profits, which makes it easier to budget. However, as you never actually own the car, leasing tends to be more expensive than buying on a monthly basis.

For example, a lease car, value of around £15,000, may cost you £400 per month, with fuel costs of £250 and insurance costs of £50. This gives you a monthly total £700. So, at the end of the year, you would be able to deduct £700 x 12 = £8400 from your profits before tax.

Buying

Now, if we take a look at how a purchase works. When you make any long-term purchase (typically to stay in your business for 1 year or more) then this becomes an asset. Assets are not deductible from your profits. Instead, you can claim the interest on the monthly payments, and then claim capital allowances on the purchase value of the asset – I go into detail about capital allowances in a couple of pages. At the time of writing, the rules for driving school cars with permanent dual controls are different than for other businesses. For most businesses, the amount you can claim may be affected by the emissions of your car, but typically you can claim 18% of the purchase price of the vehicle each year. However, driving instructors are allowed to claim up to the whole value of the car in the year of purchase, then 18% of whatever remains unclaimed in subsequent years. You can also still claim back the running costs of your car as above.

So, if we use the same figures as the first example. 18% of the £15,000 = £2700. Add to that fuel of £250 a month, £50 for insurance, and an estimate of £40 a month for interest, brings us to £6780 to deduct for the year. When you come to sell your car, if your sale price is less than the Net Book Value (the purchase price minus depreciation) then you can claim back the difference on that years set of accounts. If the sale price happens to be higher than the Net Book Value then that difference would be added to your profits meaning your tax liability for that year would be higher.

As you can see the value claimed is normally less for a purchase. However, if you purchase a new car, it will deprecate more quickly at the beginning, so it's wise to keep it for a few years to reach the break-even point in your finance. Due to the high mileage that instructors do, you may have to start paying for repairs after the first couple of years. With a lease, it is more expensive, but you'll get a new car normally every 12-18 months and any maintenance costs are covered by the lease company.

There are pros and cons to both options and sometimes it's down to personal preference of risk or security with the maintenance options. These figures are purely an example and are to be used to help you understand the different accounting methods used. Purchasing a car is a big decision, and if you make the wrong one then you'll be paying for it for a couple of years before you can change. If you are unsure then please speak to a bookkeeper or accountant and they can advise you further.

Simplified Mileage Expenses

The majority of small business owners have the choice of whether to claim the cost of their car through capital allowances (see below) along with fuel, insurance and maintenance costs OR by using simplified mileage allowance. This is where you claim an amount based on the miles that you do – the first 10,000 miles are 40p a mile, then 25p a mile after that. **Driving instructors cannot use the simplified mileage option in their business!** Many instructors, and even some accountants I've encountered, do not know that HMRC has prohibited the use of simplified mileage for instructors. This means that **all** instructors must submit their accounts using capital allowances and expenses.

Capital Allowances

Capital allowances are a minefield for even the most experienced accountants and so it is no wonder they can induce a migraine in anyone who hasn't trained in bookkeeping and accountancy! Luckily for you however, I have spent a long time getting to know capital allowances so grab yourself a coffee whilst I explain what capital allowances will mean to your business. It is worth noting, **capital allowances only apply to items you purchase.** Capital allowances therefore are not relevant if you lease your car (leases are explained in detail in the car finance section of the main book.)

HMRC normally review these allowances on a yearly basis - this information is correct at the time of writing as we look forward to the 2021-22 tax year. This is by no means a definitive tutorial and everyone's individual circumstances are different so please seek professional advice from a bookkeeper or accountant to check the information is correct for your business' circumstances before applying them to your business!

When I set up my driving school back in 2005, I assumed my tax bill would simply be the total of all of my income minus the total of all of my outgoings – who needs an accountant?!

Unfortunately, it isn't that straight forward!

There are 2 types of outgoings:

- Revenue expenditure (also known as trading expenditure) – These are costs incurred to enable you to operate within the short-term e.g. fuel costs, insurance, car valets, advertising, stationery, phone bill etc
- Capital expenditure – These are purchases expected to stay in the business for longer than 1 year, such as your driving school car.

What are capital allowances?

The nature of capital expenditure means that it is a significant cost to the business but one that will benefit the business for a long period of time (as much as we would all love to buy a brand-new car each year!).

Capital allowances therefore have been introduced to enable you to apportion your capital expenditure (cost) across a period of time to help protect your business from fluctuations in tax payments due.

Depreciation may be a term you know much better – capital allowances are in essence HMRC's way of ensuring everyone depreciates their cars (or other capital expenditure) at HMRC's 'standard' rates to avoid anyone using a clever method of depreciation to minimise the tax that they owe, as depreciation can be manipulated to suit the business.

Example:

Let's imagine you have just bought a shiny new car for £15,000.

If capital allowances didn't exist, you would simply deduct the £15,000 cost of the car from your total income which would massively reduce your tax bill in that particular year that you purchased the car.

However, the following year and the year after and the year after (and so on), you're going to have quite costly tax bills and your cash flow may take a big hit as a result (especially if you haven't invested in a bookkeeping partner who regularly advises you how much money you need to be saving to pay your tax bills at the end of each year and have therefore spent all the 'bonus tax saving' from the first year on a holiday!).

This is because you have already claimed the full value of the car in the first year and there is no car value left to deduct from your revenue in these subsequent years resulting in higher tax calculations for these years.

You'll likely still be making loan payments. However, these are not tax deductible – more on that under the car finance section – and therefore these will not help reduce the tax bill.

In addition, if you decided to stop running your own business as a driving instructor, the value of the car at this point in time (£3,000 as an example) will then be added into accounts as 'income', creating an even bigger tax bill. This is why we have capital allowances to try and smooth out the tax bills.

Types of capital allowances

There are currently 3 different types of allowances:

- Annual Investment Allowance (AIA)
- First Year Allowance (FYA)
- Written Down Allowance (WDA)

The Annual Investment Allowance (AIA)

The Annual Investment Allowance has a maximum allowance of £200,000 (as of 1st January 2021) and is reset every year. It can only be claimed in the tax year that the investment was made.

For most businesses, a car purchase would not be allowed to be claimed as an AIA, but there is a specific ruling that **driving school cars permanently fitted with dual controls can use the AIA.**

As the allowance is up to £200,000 per annum, you could claim your whole car value. However, taking the tax reduction all at once leaves you in danger of cashflow trouble in future years, just like in the example if we didn't use the allowance at all. You should liaise with your bookkeeping partner to work out how much of the AIA you should use to best support your business.

This is the great benefit of AIA – it provides you with that crucial flexibility to claim what works best for your business. For example, as new cars depreciate more in the first year than any other year, you may want to claim a little more capital allowance within the first year to match the value of the car.

You may however have more cash than anticipated at the end of the year and therefore want to use some of this cash before it burns a hole in your pocket to help reduce your tax bills in the following years. You may therefore choose to claim less AIA which will result in a higher tax bill in the year of purchase, but leave more car value left to claim against future years when cashflow may be tighter – full flexibility to make it work for your business needs at the time.

I would recommend at this point you have a chat with your bookkeeper or accountant before you make a final decision as it can have a significant impact on your future years if you don't make an informed decision. You can only use the Annual

Investment Allowance in the year of purchase so it's important you use it wisely!

Once you have decided on the amount of AIA you will claim, this gets entered onto your self-assessment tax return under the 'Annual Investment Allowance' section and is deducted from your income before calculating tax. The remaining balance gets entered into the 'general pool' which will be available to use the following year through a different allowance.

Example continued (AIA):

Your pre-tax profit the year you purchase your capital expenditure (car) is £30,000.

You decide to claim £5,000 for your car under the AIA.

This is reduced from your profit figure, resulting in taxable income of £25,000.

The remaining balance of your capital expenditure, so £10,000 in this scenario (calculated as £15,000 original cost of the car minus £5,000 claimed using AIA), is carried over to the general pool ready to use in subsequent years.

Written Down Allowance (WDA)

WDA enables you to claim up to 18% of the general pool balance per year as a capital allowance and is applied to the balance that remains in the general pool from the previous year (or any capital expenditure not eligible for AIA).

Example continued (WDA):

The general pool value carried over from the example above is £10,000.

WDA in this following year can therefore be up to £10,000 x 18% = £1800

This means that £1800 (or the value decided to be claimed if less than £1800) will be deducted from your pre-tax profit before calculating the tax due.

The remaining value (£8,200 if the full WDA is claimed) is carried forward in the general pool to the following year and the same process is repeated.

Therefore, a WDA up to £8,200 x 18% = £1476 can be claimed, leaving £6724 in the general pool for the following year if we were to claim the full WDA.

This process continues year after year until you sell the car (or take it out of the business e.g., you may gift the car to your child when you purchase a new one) or the general pool balance becomes less than £1,000 (at this point the whole balance can be deducted).

Disposal of the Asset

Firstly, no capital allowances can be claimed in the tax year that you dispose of your asset (usually a car in your business).

Instead, a disposal of asset calculation needs to be carried out to balance your capital allowance back to the original purchase price to clear down your general pool.

Even if you give your car away, for example to a family member, you must still account for the sale as if it were sold at market value even though no money has changed hands.

There are 2 common scenarios - you sell the asset and replace it or you sell the asset and don't replace it – each scenario is treated slightly differently.

Scenario 1 – you sell the asset and don't replace it (this would normally be the case if you were closing the business).

In this situation, whatever the difference is between the sale price and the amount remaining unclaimed as capital allowances is the balance.

Example 1 – You sell the car for £3000 but have £5000 of the original purchase price unclaimed. In this example you would have £2000 of unclaimed capital allowances which you could deduct from your tax earnings.

Example 2 – You sell the car for £7000 but only have £5000 of the original purchase price unclaimed. In this example you would have £2000 added onto your taxable earnings as you have claimed too much capital allowance in the previous years.

Scenario 2 – You sell the asset and replace it.

The above calculations are still true, and you may find that you have claimed more capital allowances in the previous year and need to add that to your income, or if you have not claimed the full amount then you may have additional allowances to claim for the year. However, in this situation there is more to consider….

The Annual Investment Allowance will be used for your new car as your business has invested in this new capital expenditure and so the process starts again.

Example 3 – You sell your car as in example 1 above and have £2,000 available to use as a capital allowance. You then purchase a new car for £20,000 and decided to use £5,000 of your AIA for this purchase. This means you will deduct £7,000 as capital allowances for this year from your business profit and £15,000 will be carried forward in your general pool.

Example 4 – You sell your car as in example 2 above and have a liability of £2,000. However, you purchase your new car for £20,000 and decided to use £5,000 of your AIA for this purchase. So, with an allowance of £5,000 added to your liability of £2,000, you will deduct £3,000 as capital allowance from your business profit and £15,000 will be carried forward in your general pool.

Summary

I hope this has helped you get some understanding of capital allowances, how they are applied and the importance of seeking professional advice, as using the maximum capital allowances is not always the most tax efficient thing to do and could lead to you paying out more than necessary if not done correctly. There may even be times when it is more beneficial to claim no capital allowances, for example if your earnings fall below the personal income allowance for the year or you have made a loss. I recently saved a driving instructor over £2000 as she was going to claim her full capital allowances but they would have provided her no tax saving at all due to her lower income that year. By saving it until the next tax year she can claim it when she makes more profit. If you would like any support in establishing what the best balance is for your business then please get in touch with me using the contact details at the end of the book.

Self-Assessment

As a self-employed business owner, you are required to submit a self-assessment tax return on a yearly basis. I mentioned earlier in the book that if you're registering for the first time then it must be done, at the very latest, by 5th October after the end of the tax year during which you became self-employed. The tax year runs from the 6th April to the 5th April the following year. So, for example, if you setup your business in July 2020, then you'd need to have registered by the 5th October 2021.

Your business tax year doesn't have to follow the governments tax year. You may decide to make it the anniversary of your business start date – so if you set up on the 1st June 2020, you could run it from the 1st June to 31st May. It is generally easier from an accounting point of view though to run your tax year alongside the government's tax year otherwise your accounts may fall under something called a 'basis period' and you may be taxed on your earnings twice on your first tax return. You can claim that back, but not until your business ceases trading. This is an area that is a little too in depth for the scope of this book and is something your bookkeeper can advise you on. To avoid this, most business tend to run from 6th April to 5th April, or to make things easier, it's not uncommon to run from the 1st April to 31st March. If you start your business part way through the year, e.g., 1st June, then you can end it on 5th April and file a return for the partial year, your second year will then run alongside the tax year making it easy to account for.

Following the tax year end of the 6th April you must submit your years' accounts by the latest of 31st October of the same year if submitting on paper (this is likely to be phased out in the next couple of years) or 31st January of the following year if you're submitting online. Whichever filing method you choose, the tax due must be paid in full by the 31st January as well.

E.g.

Tax Year End 5th April 2021

Paper Submission Deadline – 31st October 2021

Online Submission Deadline – 31st January 2022

Tax to be paid by – 31st January 2022

If your tax return misses the deadline, you will be charged a penalty, which will increase the longer you leave it. If you don't pay your tax on time, interest will be charged, and penalties will become due the longer it is unpaid.

There are number of planned changes proposed for self-assessment. By 2023 it is expected that Making Tax Digital will be required with the possibility of returns being needed to be submitted every quarter rather than annually. In addition, it is being discussed by the government how to make tax payable closer to the time of earning. Sometimes it can be almost 2 years from when you receive money to having to pay the tax due. As more is known about these changes I will be posting about them on my website, so please be sure to check out my latest blog posts at www.driveaheadbookkeeping.co.uk/blog

Self-assessment and your tax calculation

At the start of the chapter, I explained how your tax bill is calculated. Here, I go into more detail about how we arrive at the taxable income figure.

Profit and Loss

When your bookkeeper or accountant has completed your accounts, they will produce a profit and loss (P&L) statement and a balance sheet (see below). I've added an example on the next page (yours may look slightly different depending on the software used to create it). If you use accounting software such as Xero, you can produce your own P&L report. It summarises your income and expenditure for the year with a profit or loss total at the end – this is not your actual taxable income!

Profit and Loss
Example School of Motoring
For the year ended 31 March 2021

Account	2021
Turnover	
Lesson Income	22,000.00
Instructor Training	4,500.00
Total Turnover	**26,500.00**
Gross Profit	**26,500.00**
Administrative Costs	
Advertising	350.00
Bank Charges and Interest	900.00
Computer & Software	300.00
Miscellaneous Vehicle Expenses	620.00
Mobile Charges	850.00
Office Stationery	45.00
PPE	250.00
Printing	50.00
Subscriptions	169.00
Depreciation	2,700.00
Vehicle Fuel	3,650.00
Vehicle Insurance	480.00
Vehicle Licences	60.00
Vehicle Repair and Servicing	800.00
Web Hosting	300.00
Total Administrative Costs	**11,524.00**
Operating Profit	**14,976.00**
Other Income	
Additional Restrictions Grant	3,096.00
Sale of Assets	(820.50)
Self Employed Income Support Sche	6,000.00
Total Other Income	**8,275.50**
Profit/Loss	**23,251.50**

What does this information mean?

Turnover

The top section of the P&L report shows the business turnover for the period, which is all of the money that has come into the business during this time. If you do different types of work, for example fleet driver training, then you can separate the income into different categories if you want to. For this example, it is simply money brought in through driving lessons and instructor training.

Administrative Costs (Expenses)

The report here is produced using Xero, they label this section as administrative costs, it also commonly known as expenses. This details all of the money that has gone out of your business for the period.

Other Income

In this example I've added in income from grants and government support payments. These were payable to some businesses during the coronavirus pandemic and are included here. Hopefully the pandemic is behind us and you won't see these again in future years, but I wanted to include them so you're aware of where they would appear on your P&L.

The Sale of Asset line shows the profit (or in this case a loss as it's in brackets) when you've sold an asset from your business. For driving instructors this is normally when a car is sold. The reason there is a loss here is because the sale of the car was less than the capital allowances that were claimed, meaning the business is able to deduct the difference from their yearly profit.

Profit/Loss

At the bottom of the report, the total of all expenses is deducted from the total of the different income streams resulting in a profit or a loss. A loss would normally be identifiable as it would have brackets around it. This figure is indicative of the business for the year, but would not necessarily be the final figure for your taxable income. Some expenses may be disallowable (see below) and the P&L doesn't take into account capital allowances, these figures are adjusted afterwards.

Disallowable Expenses

I could write lists pages long of disallowable expenses, but in short, a disallowable expense is defined as *"Expenditure not incurred wholly and exclusively for trading purposes"*.

I'll give you a few examples:

Clothing – as a driving instructor you can't claim for clothes you've bought for work unless they are produced with the company logo on. You may decide you want to buy a smart shirt to work in, you can't claim for it because it is not exclusively for the use of the business, you could wear it in your personal time too.

Partial Expenses

You may use certain items for both business and personal use. Things like your mobile phone and the use of your car, may be split between home use and business use. Unlike disallowable expenses, it would be unreasonable to expect you to purchase certain items twice, one for business use and one for personal use. Any items that are split must have a record to show what percentage is used for which. Mobile phone's generally have an itemised bill so it's reasonably easy to see which is which, although a rough percentage is normally sufficient. If you use your car for personal use, then you need to keep a mileage log to record what is personal and what is business. At the end of the year then the percentage use for each will be calculated and the allowable proportion can be classed as an expense. E.g., your capital allowance for your car may work out at £2000 for the year. You record 30,000 miles driven,

22,500 of which are for business use. This means 75% was for business use so, £2000 x 75% = £1500 useable capital allowance. The same calculation may also need to be carried out for your fuel and insurance costs.

Any differences calculated here must be deducted from the relevant section of your profit and loss, or the amounts can be declared under disallowable expenses on your tax return.

Accruals and Prepayments

Accruals are expenses that have built up during your business tax year, but haven't been charged for yet. For example, the work your bookkeeper does towards your accounts may not happen until after the tax year end. But because it relates to the previous tax year, then that amount can be entered as an accrual. So, these amounts will be added to your expenses for the year.

Prepayments relate to payments made or received that aren't realised until the next tax year. If a learner pays you £300 for lessons but then only takes £100 of those lessons, then the additional £200 should be carried over to the next year. Similarly, if you've paid for your whole year of car insurance up front, then you would only claim the expense for the amounts you've used. For example, if you paid £360 for your insurance in January, you can claim for 3 months – January to March. Therefore £360 x 3/12 = £90. £90 is claimed in the current tax year, and the remaining £270 would be carried over to the following year.

Balance Sheet

A balance sheet can be produced at any time. In larger businesses it would often be monthly or quarterly. In smaller businesses, such as driving schools, they tend to be created annually on completion of the years' accounts. The balance sheet is a summary of all of your assets (what the business owns) and liabilities (what the business owes). Take a look at the balance sheet example on the next page and I'll help you to understand what it all means:

Balance Sheet
Example School of Motoring
As at 31 March 2021

Account	31 Mar 2021
Fixed Assets	
Tangible Assets	
Motor Vehicles - Cost	15,000.00
Motor Vehicles - Cost (depreciation)	(2,700.00)
Total Tangible Assets	**12,300.00**
Total Fixed Assets	**12,300.00**
Current Assets	
Cash at bank and in hand	
Bank Account	5,839.49
Total Cash at bank and in hand	**5,839.49**
Vehicle Insurance Prepayments	607.00
Total Current Assets	**6,446.49**
Creditors: amounts falling due within one year	
Prepaid Lessons Carried Over	620.00
Trade Creditors	24.99
Total Creditors: amounts falling due within one year	**644.99**
Net Current Assets (Liabilities)	**5,801.50**
Total Assets less Current Liabilities	**18,101.50**
Creditors: amounts falling due after more than one year	
Hire Purchase	12,850.00
Total Creditors: amounts falling due after more than or	**12,850.00**
Net Assets	**5,251.50**
Capital and Reserves	
Current Year Earnings	23,251.50
Drawings	(18,000.00)
Total Capital and Reserves	**5,251.50**

What does it all mean?

Fixed Assets

An asset is a resource in your business that has an economic value. Fixed assets are those that are going to remain in your business for a long time, typically more than 1 year. The most common item here will be your car but only if you own it – a lease car is never yours so would not be an asset. The depreciation figure is the estimated deprecation of the car so far. The depreciation total will increase year on year, reducing the balance of fixed assets, until you sell the car.

Current Assets

Current assets are more short-term assets and are likely to change on a regular basis. This may be money in the bank which could either be a current account or savings. Earlier on we looked at accruals – they would be recorded here. In this example, car insurance was paid upfront for the year, but towards the end of the current tax year. The remaining proportion appears under your current assets.

Creditors: amount falling due in 1 year

This is who you owe money to. As the title suggests, these are shorter term liabilities that will be repaid in less than 1 year. In this example, we can see lesson prepayments and debts the business has. Until a learner has taken the lessons that they have paid you for, they remain a liability to the business and they may need to be paid back. Any invoices that have been received, but not yet paid, also fall into this category under trade creditors.

Net Current Assets

This is simply the total of current assets minus the amount of current liabilities. Ideally you want this to be a positive figure. A negative figure would indicate that the business has too much short-term debt.

Total assets less current liabilities

Is exactly what is says. The fixed assets + the current assets – the current liabilities

Creditors: amounts falling due after more than one year

These are longer term debts. Typically, you would see loans or your car hire purchase balance here.

Net Assets

Is the total of all assets minus the total of all liabilities.

Capital and Reserves

There are 2 figures in this example:

Current year earnings are the figure from your profit and loss account.

Drawings – Unlike an employed job, your official earnings aren't known until the end of the year so you don't receive a salary. Over the course of the year, as a sole trader, you may take money out of the business for your personal use. These are called drawings.

The drawings are deducted from the current year earnings to show what is left in the business at the end of the year. If you note, this figure is the same as the net assets figure above.

What additional information is required for your self-assessment?

There are a number of different financial sources that are to be declared on your self-assessment tax return. If you received income from any of the following then it needs to be documented:

- Income you made from employment
- Interest from the bank

- Investment income
- Pensions
- Property
- Dividends

Everyone's individual circumstances are different so I'm not going to go into more detail here. If you're unsure on what needs to be declared then please get in touch with your bookkeeper or accountant.

Why use a bookkeeper or accountant?

Their role

There is some confusion about the difference between a bookkeeper and an accountant and what you require for your business. When people have asked what I do and I reply "I'm a bookkeeper", I have, on several occasions, been asked if I'm planning to open my own library at some point!

The role of a bookkeeper is to make sure all of your accounting needs are in order. Some of the tasks a bookkeeper can perform are:

- Record financial transactions (sales and expenditure)
- Produce invoices
- Reconcile your bank statements
- Manage payroll

- Make sure everything matches up in your accounts
- Complete your tax return

I personally trained with the Institute of Certified Bookkeepers (ICB) with whom I now have my practice licence. At the time of writing, I have the following qualifications:

Level 3 Certificate in Bookkeeping and Accounts

Level 3 Diploma in Payroll Management

Level 4 Certificate in Self-Assessment Taxation

This means that personally, I am qualified to perform every task that most sole traders could need. The level of support you can receive from a bookkeeper will depend on their qualifications, so don't be afraid to ask them what they are permitted to do for you. The tax affairs for a limited company are more involved than that of a sole trader. Many bookkeepers will be able to complete the majority of work required for a limited company, but may require an accountant to fulfil the requirements and reports needed by Companies House.

An accountant will analyse the figures more and will be able to help the business owner understand the impact of certain financial decisions. Accountants generally charge much more than bookkeepers, often double the amount. For the majority of driving instructors, a well-qualified bookkeeper is sufficient for their business needs.

Benefits of using a bookkeeper

I hope that this section of the book has helped you to get a good understanding of your accounts and the processes involved. Just as you give driving lessons every day, bookkeepers deal with accounts every day. It is their area of expertise and they will make sure everything is done well. By using a bookkeeper to look after your accounts you get piece of mind that everything is done correctly. They will save you time to concentrate on your business, and they will help you to get the best out of your business. Their knowledge of the ever-changing landscape that is HMRC means they will make sure you stay on the right side of the tax man, and they can help you to make better financial decisions.

Accounting Software

I did touch on this earlier in the book, but as it is finance related, I'm revisiting it here. Over the past few years, there has been an increasing rise in commercially available accounting software. The majority of software is cloud based. This means you access it through a website or via an app. The benefit of this is that you can access it anytime and anywhere. It's really easy to take a photo of a receipt on your phone which will then integrate with your accounting software. They will also integrate with your online banking so all of your transactions appear automatically. It also means that if you have other people involved in your business, such as a business partner or a bookkeeper, they can easily access the information as well.

I would highly recommend you to use cloud accounting software, my practice uses Xero. However, I'm sure you've heard the adverts from Xero and QuickBooks that tell you how easy it is to do it yourself? **It's not!!!** There is a lot you can personally do with this software, and the developments the software companies have made in recent years are fantastic, but it has its limitations if you're not a qualified professional:

- It won't tell you the correct things you can and can't claim for
- It won't calculate your depreciation for you
- It won't advise you on the best use of your capital allowances
- It cannot give tax advice (you generally need an accountant for that)

Over the next couple of years, HMRC is planning to roll out Making Tax Digital (MTD) to businesses of all sizes. This means there will be no more paper tax submissions and it may mean that your accounts will need to be submitted more frequently. Now is a great time to make a start on using cloud accounting software, so you can get to grips with it before it becomes necessary.

PART 5

HEALTH AND WELLBEING

I'm no Joe Wicks, and I certainly don't have the physique of David Beckham, but I wanted to share with you some of my experiences relating to health and wellbeing.

Driving instructors are typically an unhealthy bunch. They often work long hours, sat down for the majority of the day, and often with a poor diet. Who doesn't love a Costa midway through the day – and a cake to go with it?!

Unfortunately, I know that doesn't apply to everyone, but unfortunately it's true for a large proportion. The government recommends we all complete 10,000 steps a day. A couple of years back I had an Apple Watch and it wouldn't be uncommon for me to get to the end of the day with less than

3,000 steps completed! It's really important for us to look after ourselves - common health issues for driving instructors include:

- Weight Issues – lack of exercise and poor diet unfortunately can only mean one thing – too much excess weight.
- Back and Neck problems – being sat in a car all day, often turning to face your student or to check around the car, isn't going to do your back and neck much good. Take an opportunity wherever you can to stand. If the weather's good, then maybe stand outside the car to deliver your lesson briefing and end of lesson recap.
- Bladder issues – with a tight schedule and a scarcity of public toilets, many instructors don't go to the toilet often enough. Over time this can cause bladder issues and potentially kidney stones.
- Stress – running your own business can be stressful in itself. Some instructors don't find it stressful teaching learners; however, some do.

Life Insurance

Being a driving instructor will have an effect on your life insurance premiums, especially if you're overweight. Unfortunately, due to the above health issues, life insurance companies have recognised that you are at a greater risk and therefore more likely to claim, so have increased their premiums to reflect that. There are insurance companies who will track your health through apps or similar. These may be a better option for you if you are active as it can help to reduce your premiums.

Critical Illness Cover

Many life insurance policies have an option to add critical illness cover. This provides additional cover if you are diagnosed with a long-term or potentially terminal illness or disability. There are 30+ critical illnesses that include illnesses such as cancer, heart attacks and stroke.

Private Health Care

With increasing burdens on the NHS, many people also consider private health care. Although cover can be expensive, there are often incentives available to reduce the premium if you follow an active lifestyle. As the name suggests, private health care will provide with you faster access to medical care and testing if required. It is often provided at privately owned hospitals or clinics.

Alcohol

Being a driving instructor can be a stressful job, and
it can be easy to turn to alcohol to wind down after a
tough day at work. The adverse effects on alcohol
on your health are widely published:

- High blood pressure
- Obesity
- Heart disease
- Stroke
- Liver disease
- Increased risk of cancer

In addition to that you need consider the time that
alcohol remains in your body. A few pints the night
before you go to work can still be in your system the
following day. If you have an occasion where you
know you'll be having a drink, then keep your diary
clear the following morning (possibly the whole day
if it's going to be a big session!). Everyone knows
it's illegal to be found drink/driving, but you also
need to consider your livelihood. The DVSA would
strike you off the register with immediate effect if
you were to be found guilty of drink driving. What
would that mean for you and family? Even if you
don't get caught, your performance as a driving
instructor would be greatly reduced, as would the
respect from your pupils if they can smell alcohol in

the car. Add to that the increased chance of you being involved in accident. It's just simply not worth the risk!

If you do think alcohol is a problem for you, then don't be afraid to reach out for help from your doctor or a healthcare professional.

What can you do to improve your health?

Just walk!

The easiest and most accessible form of exercise for most people is to go for a walk. Experts have shown that just a 30 minute walk every day can have excellent health benefits. Schedule some time in your day. Whether it's before or after work, or maybe set some time mid-way through your day. It'll be good to get out of the car, stretch your legs and give your body a break from being sat down.

Join a gym or a club/team

I know several instructors that like to get to the gym first thing in the morning and find it a great way to start their day. I know a lot of people couldn't think of anything worse. The great thing is there are so many opportunities for you to get healthy. Did you have a sport at school that you particularly liked? There are plenty of senior clubs around the country that would welcome you back into a sport. Being part of a team can be a great motivation to get moving, but more importantly to continue being active well into the future.

A couple of years back I joined a local running club. I had previously run, on and off, for a number of years but struggled to keep it going. The club had groups for every ability and were massively welcoming to me. It was great to get out there, be active and engage with other people, and that's what kept me going. Since the coronavirus lockdowns, I haven't got back into running with the club yet, but that habit has stuck with me and I still continue to run at least 3 times a week.

The important thing is – just do something. If you can just start to do a little bit a couple of times a week to start to form the habit, you'll find that the more you do, the more you want to do!

Meditation and Mindfulness

It's very easy to let the everyday grind get you down and for stress to build up. Meditation used to be seen as a bit woo woo, and was only for pony tailed hippies who sat crossed legged chanting. It's really not like that, and is very easy to get into. There are lots of online resources and apps to get you started.

I've used the Calm app for a little while, and it starts with just 10-minute daily sessions. There's also an app called Headspace. I've not used it personally, but they recently released a programme on Netflix to help people get into and understand mindfulness. Give it a try, you'll see the benefits really quickly, and it's amazing how just 10 minutes can help you to relax and get a different focus on the day.

Summary

I really hope you've enjoyed reading this book and that you can take the subjects discussed and apply them to your business. It's very easy to read a book like this, get some good ideas and feel very positive about how you can implement them into your business, but then within a week, forget all about it and do nothing.

It may be a good idea to re-read the book and mark out the sections that will benefit you. Then when you write your 7-day, 30-day and 90-day plans, think about how you can put these practices and ideas into your business.

I'd love to hear your comments about this book. Has it helped you get a better understanding of your business? Are there things you'd like to know more about? Or would you like some bookkeeping assistance? Please get in touch using my website and social media links:

www.driveaheadbookkeeping.co.uk

www.facebook.com/driveaheadbookkeeping

www.linkedin.com/in/drive-ahead-bookkeeping/

Or why not give me a call on 01782 906001

Printed in Great Britain
by Amazon